Billy Graham Evangelistic Association

Dear Friend,

I am pleased to provide you with this copy of *Hope for the Troubled Heart*, by my father, Billy Graham.

My father first published this book in 1991, but his words are just as timely today as they were then. Where can you find hope when life seems to crumble around you? By looking to the Bible, my father explains how you can meet God in the midst of pain—and discover a peace that will never be shaken.

The Billy Graham Evangelistic Association exists to take the message of Christ to all we can by every effective means available to us. Our desire is to introduce as many people as we can to the person of Jesus Christ, so that they might experience His love and forgiveness.

Your prayers are the most important way to support us in this ministry. We are grateful for the dedicated prayer support we receive. We are also grateful for those who support us with contributions.

If you would like to know more about the Billy Graham Evangelistic Association, please contact us:

In the U.S.:

Billy Graham Evangelistic Association
1 Billy Graham Parkway
Charlotte, North Carolina 28201-0001
www.billygraham.org
Toll-free: 1-877-2GRAHAM
(1-877-247-2426)

In Canada:

Billy Graham Evangelistic Association of Canada
20 Hopewell Way NE
Calgary, Alberta T3J 5H5
www.billygraham.ca
Toll-free: 1-888-393-0003

We would appreciate knowing how this book or our ministry has touched your life. May God bless you.

Sincerely,

Franklin Graham
President

STEPS TO PEACE WITH GOD

1. RECOGNIZE GOD'S PLAN—PEACE AND LIFE

   The message in this book stresses that God loves you and wants you to experience His peace and life.

   The BIBLE says ... For God loved the world so much that He gave His only Son, so that everyone who believes in Him may not die but have eternal life. John 3:16

2. REALIZE OUR PROBLEM—SEPARATION

   People choose to disobey God and go their own way. This results in separation from God.

   The BIBLE says ... Everyone has sinned and is far away from God's saving presence. Romans 3:23

   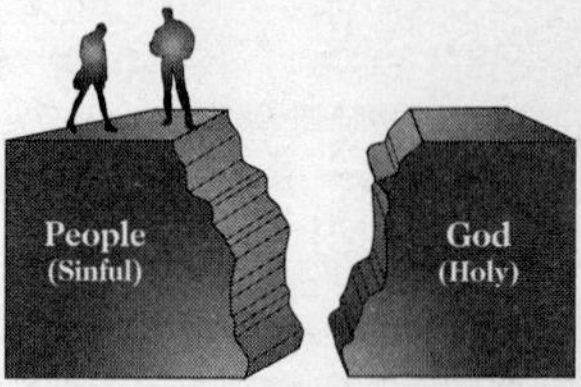

3. RESPOND TO GOD'S REMEDY—CROSS OF CHRIST

   God sent His Son to bridge the gap. Christ did this by paying the penalty of our sins when He died on the cross and rose from the grave.

   The BIBLE says ... But God has shown us how much He loves us—it was while we were still sinners that Christ died for us! Romans 5:8

4. RECEIVE GOD'S SON—LORD AND SAVIOR

   You cross the bridge into God's family when you ask Christ to come into your life.

   The BIBLE says ... Some, however, did receive Him and believed in Him; so He gave them the right to become God's children. John 1:12

   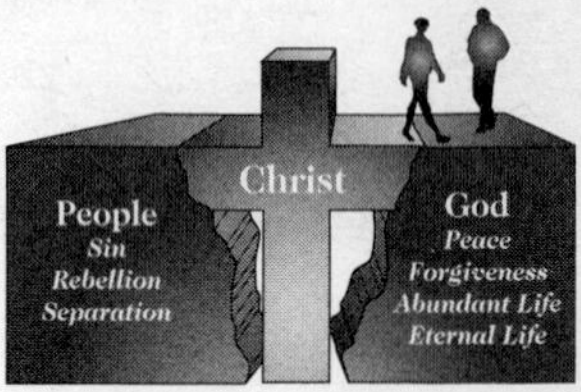

THE INVITATION IS TO:

REPENT (turn from your sins) and by faith RECEIVE Jesus Christ into your heart and life and follow Him in obedience as your Lord and Savior.

PRAYER OF COMMITMENT

"Lord Jesus, I know I am a sinner. I believe You died for my sins. Right now, I turn from my sins and open the door of my heart and life. I receive You as my personal Lord and Savior. Thank You for saving me now. Amen."

If you are committing your life to Christ, please let us know!
Billy Graham Evangelistic Association
1 Billy Graham Parkway, Charlotte, NC 28201-0001
1-877-2GRAHAM (1-877-247-2426)
www.billygraham.org

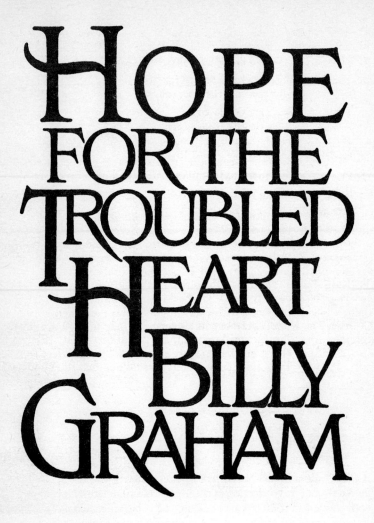

HOPE FOR THE TROUBLED HEART

BILLY GRAHAM

This **Billy Graham Library Selection** *is published by the Billy Graham Evangelistic Association with permission from W Publishing Group, a division of Thomas Nelson, Inc.*

W PUBLISHING GROUP™
www.wpublishinggroup.com
A Division of Thomas Nelson, Inc.
www.ThomasNelson.com

HOPE FOR THE TROUBLED HEART

Published by the Billy Graham Evangelistic Association with permission from W Publishing Group, a division of Thomas Nelson, Inc.

A *Billy Graham Library Selection* designates materials that are appropriate for a well-rounded collection of quality Christian literature, including both classic and contemporary reading and reference materials.

ISBN 1–59328–093–9
Previous ISBNs 0–8499–0702–0
0–8499–4211–x (pbk.)

Contents

Foreword

In my travels over the decades, I have found that people are the same the world over. However, in recent years I find that there is an increasing problem that I would sum up in the word "hopeless." It may be because we get news of troubles, problems, disasters, wars, etc. instantaneously in comparison to years ago when it might have taken weeks, months, or even years to hear of an event. But there's something else even more insidious. People in the most affluent societies are feeling this sense of despair and hopelessness.

Perhaps the greatest psychological, spiritual, and medical need that all people have is the need for hope. Dr. McNair Wilson, the famous cardiologist, remarked in his autobiography, *Doctor's Progress,* "Hope is the medicine I use more than any other—hope can cure nearly anything."

I remember years ago that Dr. Harold Wolff, professor of medicine at Cornell University Medical College and associate professor of psychiatry, said, "Hope, like faith and a purpose in life, is medicinal. This is not exactly a statement of belief, but a conclusion proved by meticulously controlled scientific experiment."

Hope is both biologically and psychologically vital to man. Men and women must have hope, and yet a great part of our world today is living without it. The Apostle Paul wrote two thousand years ago to the Ephesians that the Roman civilization of his day was "without hope."

This is like so much of our world today. We are trying to live normal lives without ultimate hope, and we are finding failures on every hand. I believe that *Hope for the Troubled Heart,* which I have written with the help of several other people, will not only be of help but will be life-transforming for many who may read it. I send it forth with a prayer that it will bring new hope to thousands of sufferers from this terrible disease of hopelessness.

This book has been written with the help especially of my longtime friend Carole Carlson; my beloved wife, Ruth, who seems to have unlimited resources for every subject that I write on; my friend Millie Dienert, who was kind enough to go through the manuscript and make suggestions while on our way to Moscow recently; and to my wonderful, small staff at Montreat, especially Stephanie Wills who typed and retyped changes in the manuscript. For their patience, I want to thank Word Publishing, who waited many long months while I finished the book in the midst of other pressing demands.

May God bless this volume to the encouragement of thousands and give hope to the despairing.

Billy Graham
Europe, Summer of 1991

1

World in Pain

VOICES FROM TROUBLED HEARTS: "Our home is a war zone! Don't talk to me about international war. I want to know how we can find peace in our family!" . . . "I'm a rape victim. How can I ever get over my memories, or my horrible fears?" . . . "I've lost my job and may lose my home. Don't tell me about Wall Street blues!" . . . "How can I raise decent kids when they're surrounded by bad influences?" . . . "I'm more worried about what's polluting the minds of my children. They're the most endangered species!" . . . "We have a nice home and cars—you'd think I would be happy. But I feel empty. I'm not sure of my husband anymore and I'm so lonely."

"This is the generation that will pass through the fire. It is the generation . . . 'under the gun.' This is the tormented generation. This is the generation destined to live in the midst of crisis, danger, fear, and death. We are like a people under sentence of death, waiting for the date to be set. We sense that something is about to happen. We know that things cannot go on as they are. History has reached an impasse. We are now on a collision course. Something is about to give."

I wrote this in 1965.

At that time few of us thought the world could get much worse and survive. I was wrong. In many ways the world has gotten worse, and we have survived. But we are a world in pain—a world that suffers collectively from the violence of nature and man, and a world that suffers individually from personal heartache.

Because we have instant communication today, our planet has shrunk to the size of a television screen. Although husbands and wives, children and parents, have trouble communicating, we can watch a war as it is happening before our eyes. A comfortable room can be turned into a foreign battlefield or a street riot with the push of a button.

Our children have grown and married and we now have (at last count) nineteen grandchildren. I cannot promise them that this present world will get better. With all my heart, I would like to protect them from pain. But what I see is a universal malaise which affects civilization, giving me little hope that man alone can change the course of human events to make a better world.

There have been dazzling achievements in the years since my children were small. Man has landed on the moon, and Patriot missiles have intercepted and destroyed incoming ballistic warheads. From world records in sports to VCR's and microwave ovens, this has been a period of great scientific change.

But how far have we come? Are we better off in the nineties than we were in the sixties? In 1965 I said that most of the current experts, analysts, philosophers, and statesmen agreed that man is sick. Some of them believed we had already passed the point of no return. Has the patient improved or is the diagnosis terminal?

Pain of Wars

We are told by historians that peace has never been achieved at any time in history. Since the early eighteenth century, the world has known only eleven years in which there have been no wars. Even during those eleven years, there may have been small undetected wars in out-of-the-way places in the world.

In 1982 I was invited to address a peace conference in Moscow. After much agony, seeking advice from different people that I trust, but primarily the advice of Scripture, I decided to go. I took a great deal of criticism, but God used it to open many doors in Eastern Europe, which I believe was a contributing factor to the vast changes in the Soviet Union. The speech that I gave there, which was based on the teachings of Scripture concerning peace and war, was quoted over and over throughout the Eastern world.

> "*But how far have we come?*
> *Are we better off in the nineties than we were in the sixties?*
> *Has the patient improved or is the diagnosis terminal?*"

The United Nations proclaimed 1986 as the International Year of Peace. What happened? The world responded with more than a hundred wars, according to the Center for Defense Information in Washington.

Despite the overwhelming evidence that the absence of peace may be the norm, rather than the exception, one newsman said in December 1989, "Peace on earth seems more possible now than at any time since World War II." This was a hopeful note in a war-weary world, but since then we have had the Persian Gulf War and many other little wars.

Augustine, in the fourth century, believed that achievement of an absolute state of peace on earth was impossible and that war would always claim its place. The weight of history favors Augustine's view over that of the optimistic newsman.

Pain of Lawlessness

Violent crime, often linked with the war against drugs, has accelerated. From every city in the world come stories of drug-related shootings, stabbings, and assaults. A doctor in a Detroit hospital said that the saddest casualties are children. "We have a whole generation of human beings within this urban area who could be so productive and helpful to humanity but are being lost. We have kids thirteen and fourteen years old who are as hardened as anyone in a penitentiary. Look into their eyes, and you see these cold blank stares, void of most moral values."[1]

In Los Angeles, police make drug arrests at a rate of over a thousand a week—and that's less than one-fourth of what they think the real story is. "Despite the passage of tough anti-drug laws and police dragnets, street crime, much of it drug-related, continues to surge. The nation's violent-crime rate rose 10 percent in the first six months of 1990. Murders were up 8 percent in the first six months of the year and armed robbery rose 9 percent."[2] An FBI report showed that in the last few years, arrests for drug-abuse violations rose dramatically and dangerously.

I love New York and have many friends there, but the stories from that city are heartbreaking. It is reported as having 500,000 drug abusers, an amount almost equal to the population of Boston. In 1952, the city had 8,757 robberies. In 1989 there were 93,387! *U.S. News & World Report* stated in 1990, "Twenty-one cabbies were murdered this year, girls were raped and then thrown off rooftops, a boy was tied up and set afire, and four small children were shot to death in drug wars within three weeks."[3]

> *Part of our problem with debt is that we have confused needs with wants. Yesterday's luxuries are today's necessities.*

Lawlessness is not confined to the city streets. Most law-enforcement officers say the most dangerous calls are those related to domestic arguments. Beatings, rapes, and murder are also happening behind the white picket fences of our suburbs and small towns.

Random violence, without any provocation or reason, is everywhere. No one is safe. We are a nation living behind fences and bars—not only in America, but also in the United Kingdom, Brazil, and many other countries.

Pain of Economic Collapse

Fraud is rampant wherever we are. In the financial world, the cheating touches many of our pocketbooks. When a large savings-and-loan institution collapsed, the American taxpayers probably ended up paying some $2 billion in additional taxes.

Real estate values have so many ups and downs that the financial institutions struggle with bad loans. Is there any doubt that we are a nation in debt?

Part of our problem with debt is that we have confused needs with wants. Yesterday's luxuries are today's necessities.

One of Wall Street's most notorious insider traders summed up this materialistic idolatry in a speech to graduate business school students when he claimed, "Greed is good for you." It wasn't so good for this man, who soon found himself the target of federal indictments for alleged wrongdoing.

"Dark Mood" announced a *Wall Street Journal* headline. The infection spreads, as crisis feeds on itself and fears are expressed for everything from bank failures to global financial panic.

Pain of Family Failure

No subject is closer to my heart than the family. Sometimes I feel that my heart will break when I see the results of divorce, infidelity, and rebellion. The moral foundation of our country is in danger of crumbling as families break up and parents neglect their responsibilities. Isn't it ironic that people cheer and clap for couples who have been married for more than twenty-five years? On a television talk show I announced that my wife and I have been married for nearly fifty years, and we are more in love than ever. The applause was deafening. People seemed surprised, because it is so unusual.

The results of family disintegration are seen all around us. Runaways. Child abuse. Abortions. It is dirty laundry—once hung in the nation's backyard, but now hung shamelessly in front yards—flaunted in headlines and glamorized on television and in films.

One result of family failure has been the loss of dignity. No better example can be found than in the use of language. It's a four-letter world in movies, on television, in comedy routines, and in real life. *Time* magazine asks, "Are the '90s destined to be the Filth Decade?"[4]

Most decent people wonder what impact the raw-language culture will have on this first generation to grow up with it. Music and comedy routines flout human decency in such obscene ways that even reading about them makes us sick.

Are we shock-proof? Parents may still be capable of open-mouthed dismay, but today's youth seems unshockable. This in itself is shocking!

A news commentator said, "Since the traumas of the Kennedy assassination and Vietnam, many Americans have gradually closed off their minds to the nature of atrocity. They cope with the world's horror by numbing themselves to pain. They can shed tears over cute, tender stories of stranded whales or a baby in a well, but all too often everything else—from a politician's promise to the Chernobyl disaster—is so much show biz, ironized with shrugs and sick jokes. Today's children were bred in this atmosphere. With many of their parents past caring, how can the kids not be past shock?"[5]

Pain of a Ravished Earth

The 1990s are appearing to be the decade of environmental concerns. After years of polluting our air and water with little thought about the consequences, many are now trying to be good stewards of the earth that God gave us. Global warming, holes in the ozone layer, tainted water supplies, choking smog layers, and overflowing landfills are just a small part of the concerns.

Over twenty years ago, at a time when environment meant simply the surroundings in which we lived and not an endangered species, Francis Schaeffer wrote in *Pollution and the Death of Man:* "The simple fact is that if man is not able to solve his ecological problems, then man's resources are going to die. . . . So the whole problem of ecology is dumped in this generation's lap."[6]

The problem has truly been dumped upon us. We have made some strides toward its solution, but this ravished earth is like the man who smoked all of his life without any consequences, until one day lung cancer was discovered. Our natural resources have been misused for too many generations, and we are paying the price.

Pain of Affluence

Someone has said that Americans have more wealth, more two-car families, more private homes, and write more books on how to be happy than any other country. If we lived in Bangladesh or in the slums of Calcutta, the thought of suffering in the midst of abundance would sound ridiculous. And yet in America, where the standard of living is one of the highest in the world, the very presence of a life of comparative ease causes a spiritual sickness. A letter from one of the workers for Samaritan's Purse, which provides help for hurting people throughout the world and is headed by my son Franklin, illustrates how affluence can be painful. He wrote:

> One day I was in one of the large camps where Indian nationals from Kuwait were being held waiting repatriation. These people had traveled for days across the burning desert in buses. I noticed a lady with her family of small children who was very distressed, and when I went to her I found that she had given birth to a baby three days before being evacuated from Kuwait. The baby was so dirty and smelly. It was great to be able to buy her all that was needed for the baby,

as well as helping the mother with some of her urgent medical problems. The mother's gratitude was profound, and on further conversation with her we found that she had once walked with the Lord. The affluence of living in Kuwait had come between her and God, and her love for Him had grown cold. As we shared with her God's willingness to forgive her, she found new fellowship with Him and was rejoicing in His comfort and care as we left her.

Almost the last thing she said to me was, "I just thank God for allowing my family to lose everything in Kuwait so I could find Him again."

"

Materialism may do what a foreign invader could never hope to achieve—materialism robs a nation of its spiritual strength.

"

My wife was talking with a young Christian who had just arrived in this country from a regime hostile to Christianity. The woman was suffering from culture shock. She told Ruth, "I think it is more difficult to remain a deeply committed Christian in the midst of prosperity than under persecution."

Materialism may do what a foreign invader could never hope to achieve—materialism robs a nation of its spiritual strength.

Seen or Unseen Pain

In every country and city throughout the world there are people who are suffering from personal pain. Some of it is visible, like the legless war veteran—some is intensely private, like the woman who has lived with the memory of childhood rape.

In my years of global travels, I have seen a world in pain. Some people seem to have more of their share than others. Many can't understand why suffering is their lot.

When Aleksandr Solzhenitsyn described the horrors of torture and death in his book, *The Gulag Archipelago*, a study of the Soviet network of prisons during the Stalin era, he expressed a universal question for all sufferers—"The most sophisticated and the veriest simpleton among us, drawing on all life's experience can gasp out only: 'Me? What for?'"[7]

Me? What For?

When suffering hits us personally, that is the common cry. *Why Me? What's the reason?*

For man without faith in a personal God, reactions to painful situations are as varied as pain itself. In a news release about the deposed Kuwaiti leaders attempting to conduct a government in exile after being ousted from their country by the Iraqi invasion, there was a story of a doctor who had left Kuwait and gone to Egypt. His friend, another Kuwaiti exile, said, "He locked his door and grew his beard, and he did not come out, he just lay on the bed looking at the ceiling. He did not talk to anybody. Probably he saw strange things. When we go back to Kuwait, I think we should bring hundreds of psychiatrists."[8]

The doctor from Kuwait is like many who respond to suffering by retreating into a private world without any solution. Others find bizarre methods of escape. After a serious operation a Hollywood actress was told by her doctor to meditate with pieces of quartz as a therapy to reduce stress.[9]

Without God's guidance, our response to suffering is a futile attempt to find solutions to conditions that cannot be solved. We are plummeting into a world where, in spite of wonder drugs and medical breakthroughs, suffering will become more intense. For all suffering, we know, is not physical. Today, more than ever, we need to know how to find strength to live life to its fullest.

Mirror of Despair

Personal pain has been with us since God told Eve she would have pain in childbirth. However, in spite of the wars and plagues of the past, there has never been a time when a mirror on the world has reflected so much despair.

"*Today, more than ever, we need to know how to find strength to live life to its fullest.*"

In 1965, I wrote that the flames of lawlessness, racial unrest, political dilemma, and immorality were out of control. How can I describe that blaze today? It's like the oil wells burning in Kuwait. "Looks like Hell," one observer said. Compared with the 1990s, the 1960s, for all of their rebellion and turmoil, seem almost quaint and placid.

Nothing seems to satisfy. Not politics, not education, not material goods. Some who refuse to turn their hearts toward God have created the New Age movement, with all of its aberrations. This is actually not new but only the latest attempt by man to place something other than Christ inside himself in a futile attempt to satisfy spiritual longings.

As men and women seek to find independence from God, they have lost a sense of purpose in life. The worth of human personality is often equated with what we do for a living. However, a person's occupation, community standing, or bank account is not what is important in God's eyes.

Not only do many not know God, but those who do rarely listen to His voice. It is a tragedy that many of God's people have conformed themselves to the world and its thinking, rather than being transformed by the renewing of their minds. We have become a nation of biblical illiterates. A Gallup survey found that although 90 percent of Americans own Bibles, only 11 percent of Christians read the Bible daily.

As mankind sees its reflection, it is not a pretty sight.

Walking Through the Rubble

While individual suffering has no respite and the collective suffering of our world continues, there are those who have found a refuge in the midst of the rubble. What is the difference between the paraplegic woman with the smile that lights a room and the millionaire with a suicide wish? Or what makes one person accept and keep his balance during a painful time, and another become a self-pitying whiner?

Outside of the Bible, I cannot offer true, unfailing solutions. I do not pretend to be a pop-psychologist or offer pat answers. An old Scottish writer said: "The 'household of faith' has many concerns, and not the least of these are its sorrows. These are the lot of all; and there is no member of the household but has his share in these, either in personal suffering or in helping to bear the burden of others."[10]

We can react with bitterness and hate God, as some do, or we can accept suffering as a natural part of life and a condition that comes with living in this world. We cannot avoid suffering, but we can determine our response to it.

It is my prayer that many voices from troubled hearts may find peace in this world of pain and hope in the midst of hopeless situations.

2

His Unfailing Love

A unit joined to infinity adds nothing to it, any more than one foot added to infinite length. The finite is annihilated in the presence of God and becomes pure zero. So is our intellect before God.

Blaise Pascal

AS A LITTLE BOY GROWING UP IN THE SOUTH, my idea of the ocean was very small. The first time I saw the Atlantic I couldn't imagine that any lake could be so big! The vastness of the oceans cannot be understood until they are seen. This is the same with God's love; it is incomprehensible until you actually experience it. No one can describe its wonders to you.

For years Ruth had been trying to secure the release of the last two members of a family still living in the People's Republic of China. The young widowed mother was in America, but her son and daughter had not been able to get out of China.

Ruth and her two sisters and brother were on their way to their old home in China in 1980, but before leaving she made one final call to the State Department to see if the arrangements had been finished for their trip. She was saddened to find out there was no good news for the young mother about her children. They were not granted permits to leave the country and come to America.

My wife stopped in California to see the woman and other members of the family who had escaped. It was then that the lovely young mother told Ruth this story.

There was once in China a kind seller of cherries. A little boy came along, and when he saw the fruit his eyes filled with longing. He had no money, but the seller of cherries asked, "Do you want some cherries?" Of course, he did. But he only ducked his head shyly.

The kind seller of cherries said, "Hold out your hands." But the little boy kept his hands at his sides. The seller said again, "Hold out your hands." The little boy still stood stiffly. The man reached down and gently took the child's hands. Cupping them together, he filled them with cherries.

Later the boy's mother asked, "Why didn't you hold out your hands when he asked you?" The little boy answered, "Because his hands were bigger than mine." Then the mother smiled. "His hands are bigger than ours," she said. "We can wait."

That Chinese family is now reunited in California. Truly, God's hands are bigger than ours, and He is able to fill them to overflowing.

What Is God Like?

Some see God as a harsh father, waiting to punish His children when they do something wrong. Others perceive God as unable to handle the evil on earth, or indifferent to the suffering caused by it.

God's love is unchangeable; He knows exactly what we are and loves us anyway. In fact, He created us because He wanted other creatures in His image upon whom He could pour out His love and who would love Him in return. He also wanted that love to be voluntary, not forced, so He gave us freedom of choice, the ability to say yes or no in our relationship to Him. God does not want mechanized love, the kind that says we must love God because it's what our parents demand or our church preaches. Only voluntary love satisfies the heart of God.

Years ago a friend of mine was standing on top of a mountain in North Carolina and noticed two cars in the distance heading toward each other on a dangerously winding road. He realized neither driver could see the other car approaching. With horror, he watched a third car pull up and begin to pass one of the cars as all three entered a blind curve. My friend shouted a warning, even though he knew he couldn't be heard. The crash was fatal and several were killed. The man standing on the mountain saw it all.

> *God's love is unchangeable; He knows exactly what we are and loves us anyway.*

God is a God of love, and He is not blind to man's plight. He doesn't stand on a mountaintop, viewing the wrecks in our lives, without shouting a warning. Since man caused his own crash by his rebellion against the Creator, God could have allowed him to plunge into destruction.

From the very beginning of man's journey, God had a plan for man's deliverance. In fact, the plan is so fantastic that it ultimately lifts each man who will accept His plan far above even the angels. God's all-consuming love for mankind was decisively demonstrated at the cross, where His *compassion* was embodied in His Son, Jesus Christ. The word compassion comes from two Latin words meaning "to suffer with." God was willing to suffer with man.

In His thirty-three years on earth, Jesus suffered with man; on the cross He suffered for man. "God was reconciling the world to himself in Christ" (2 Corinthians 5:19). An important verse to memorize is: "God demonstrates His own love for us in this: While we were still sinners, Christ died for us" (Romans 5:8).

God's love did not begin at the cross. It began in eternity before the world was established, before the time clock of civilization began to move. The concept stretches our minds to their utmost limits.

Can you imagine what God was planning when the earth was "without form and void"? There was only a deep, silent darkness of outer space that formed a vast gulf before the brilliance of God's throne. God was designing the mountains and the seas, the flowers and the animals. He was planning the bodies of His children and all their complex parts.

How could creation be by chance?

Even before the first dawn, He knew all that would happen. In His mysterious love He allowed it. The Bible tells us about the "Lamb that was slain from the creation of the world" (Revelation 13:8). God foresaw what His Son was to suffer. It has been said there was a cross in the heart of God long before the cross was erected at Calvary. As we think about it we will be overwhelmed at the wonder and greatness of His love for us.

That Amazing Love

God's love liberated man from the beginning of time to do his own thing, but whatever his choice, there were to be either benefits or consequences. Adam and Eve enjoyed the benefits for a while, but they forced every generation that would ever be born to face the consequences.

It was the love of God which put the Ten Commandments in the hands of His servant, Moses. It was His love which engraved those laws, not only in stone, but also upon the hearts of all people. Those commandments became the foundation of all civil, statutory, and moral law and the basis of conscience. It was God's love which knew that men were incapable of obeying His law, and it was His love which promised a Redeemer, a Savior, who would save His people from their sins.

"*I believe that God in His love is preparing us now for the Second Coming of Christ, and that time may be nearer than we think.*"

It was the love of God which put words of promise into the mouths of His prophets, centuries before Christ came to this planet. It was God's love that planned the political conditions before the coming of Jesus Christ. Greece, as the great power during the four-hundred-year period before the birth of Christ, prepared the way for His message by spreading a common language throughout the world. Then the transportation problem had to be solved, and the great Roman Empire came into power and built a network of roads and developed a system of law and order. So by using the common language and the Roman roads and legal system, God spread His Word through the early Christians. The Scripture says that "when the time had fully come, God sent his Son" (Galatians 4:4).

I believe that God in His love is preparing us now for the Second Coming of Christ, and that time may be nearer than we think.

Like Father, Like Son

The greatest tribute a boy can give to his father is to say, "When I grow up I want to be just like my dad." It is a convicting responsibility for us fathers and grandfathers. Not too long ago I received a handwritten letter from my youngest son, Ned. It is a letter I will always prize. He expressed his appreciation and love for me as his father, and he indicated that he hoped he would be a good role model for his two sons and that he would be able to impact them the way I had been able to impact him. This encouraged me, because I have felt I was a failure as a father due to my extensive absences from home. But Ruth was strong enough and spiritual enough to be both father and mother at the times the children needed it. When I did come home, I tried to spend extra time with them. Now I face the problems and opportunities of trying to be a good grandfather for nineteen grandchildren. Our lives speak loudly to those around us, especially the children in our home.

The Son of God reflects the same selfless compassion for the sick, the distressed, and the sin-burdened as does God the Father. It was God's love which enabled Jesus to become poor, that we might become rich. It was divine love that enabled Him to endure the cross. It was this same love that restrained Him when He was falsely accused of blasphemy and led to Golgotha to die with common thieves.

When a boy is picked on by a bully, he might call for his big brother or his dad to help him. When I was in grammar school, I was constantly being picked on by a bully who must have weighed one-third more than I did. This older boy went out of his way to give me a beating almost every day. One day as we were getting on the school bus and he was slapping me around, a tiny little guy came up and knocked the daylights out of the bully! My defender had taken boxing, wrestling, and karate lessons, and he gave the other boy a sound thrashing. From then on, all three of us were friends.

I remember when my brother, Melvin, was small, and he was picked on by some older boys in our town. I was bigger then and had the chance to defend him.

Jesus could have called on a host of angels to defend Him. They could have drawn their swords and come to His rescue at any time. But His love held Him on the cross and made Him, in a moment of agonizing pain, stop and give hope to a repentant sinner dying beside Him who said, "'Jesus, remember me when you come into your kingdom.' Jesus answered him, 'I tell you the truth, today you will be with me in paradise'" (Luke 23:42–43).

After terrible torture had been inflicted upon Him by degenerate man, it was love that caused Him to lift His voice and pray, "Father, forgive them, for they do not know what they are doing" (Luke 23:34).

From Genesis to Revelation, from earth's greatest tragedy to earth's greatest triumph, the dramatic story of man's lowest depths and God's most sublime heights can be expressed in twenty-five tremendous words: "For God so loved the world, that he gave his only begotten Son, that whosoever believeth in him should not perish, but have everlasting life" (John 3:16 KJV).

How Can We Comprehend His Love?

On the human level, we frequently love the one who loves us. In the spiritual realm, people do not grasp the overwhelming love of a holy God, but we can understand God's love by getting to know Him through Jesus Christ. No one can grasp the love of the God of the universe without knowing His Son.

Lloyd Ogilvie tells about a conversation with an old friend who said, "Lloyd, I've been a closet agnostic for some time now.

I used to be so sure of what I believed, but now I have to admit I've known about God, but never really known God. I've got so many unanswered questions. I guess my mind has finally caught up with my heart."

Ogilvie continues, "Agnosticism is the silent agony of our age. It's not questions about God's existence that trouble most people, but questions about what He is like and how they can know Him. The unanswered questions about God, about His nature, will and ways have surfaced as an honest but very unsatisfying, 'I just don't know!' And this uncertainty troubles people both inside and outside the church."[1]

Speak about the love of God and faces light up, but speak of God as a Judge, and our attitudes change. But God is the Judge of His world; as our Maker, He owns us. He is a Judge who loves righteousness and hates sin, and He is always just.

If we are unfortunate enough to stand before a judge in a court of law, we hope that he or she is fair. God's judgments are based on His wisdom, which is wiser than those of men.

We are not unlike the writer of Psalm 73, who saw the prosperity of the wicked and complained, "They have no struggles, their bodies are healthy and strong. They are free from the burdens common to man." A common cry is "Why do evil men prosper and good men suffer?" In the seventeenth century, John Trapp wrote, "Envy not such a one his prosperity, any more than you would a corpse his flowers."

God is not indifferent to right and wrong. The judgment of a Holy God is as much a part of His nature as His love for us. Judgment means that in the end God's will will be perfectly done. We hear, "How can God love me when I have lived such a despicable life?" "How can God love the world when there is so much needless suffering?" You may have questions of your own which begin with "How can God love . . . ?"

No matter what sin we have committed, no matter how terrible it may be, God loves us.

What God's Love Can't Do

God cannot forgive the unrepentant sinner. The human race is called on throughout the Bible to repent of sin and return to God. This love of God can be entirely rejected. God will not force Himself upon any man against his will. A person can hear a message about the love of God and say, "No, I won't have it," and God will let him go on in his sin to eternity without God.

Francis Schaeffer wrote, "So often people think that Christianity is only something soft, only a kind of gooey love that loves evil equally with good. This is not the biblical position. The holiness of God is to be exhibited simultaneously with love."[2]

> *"No matter what sin we have committed, no matter how terrible it may be, God loves us."*

When I think about God's love I tend to dwell upon all the good and great things He has done for me. Then I must stop and realize that even when circumstances don't look too bright, God's love still shines. I cannot hide from His love, nor can I escape it.

Shortly after my mother's companion, Rose Adams, lost her husband, Mother wrote a note to her. She said: "Dear precious one: When this storm shall pass, the brightness for which He is preparing you will appear unclouded and it shall be Himself."

No Place to Hide

Escapism seems to be the order of the day. Escape by travelling, go to another city or another country and life will be better. Escape with drugs or alcohol, and the bitterness of living will be blurred. Escape into hobbies or work or television. Reality is too harsh.

We can't escape from God. In Psalm 139:1–5, David said, "O Lord, you have searched me and you know me. You know when I sit and when I rise; you perceive my thoughts from afar. You discern my going out and my lying down; you are familiar with all my ways. Before a word is on my tongue you know it completely, O Lord. You hem me in, behind and before; you have laid your hand upon me."

God's love is called by that theological term *omniscient.* David could not explain the manner of that kind of love any more than we can. However, he could tell how it affected him: "Such knowledge is too wonderful for me, too lofty for me to attain" (v. 6). He goes on to acknowledge that God is in every place. "Where can I go from your presence? If I go up to the heavens, you are there; if I make my bed in the depths, you are there" (vv. 7–8).

If one could climb to the highest heights or descend to the lowest depths, one could not escape the presence of Almighty God. This is what the omniscience and the omnipresence of God means to us in practical terms. "If I rise on the wings of the dawn, if I settle on the far side of the sea, even there your hand will guide me, your right hand will hold me fast" (Psalm 139:9–10).

Every day I read a Psalm to give me strength for the day and a realization of the power of God's love. His love has seen me through sickness, discouragement, and frustration. His love has sustained me during times of disappointment and bewilderment. However, I have never experienced some of the terrible trials of some of my fellow Christians. I have never been in prison or physically tortured for my faith, but I have known those who have been.

In 1948 a Rumanian Christian pastor was taken prisoner by the Communists. For sixteen years he was moved from one camp to another, brutally beaten, drugged, and tortured. He underwent brainwashing of the most diabolical kind, but his faith held strong. After years of imprisonment, he almost reached the breaking point. The prisoners were given postcards to invite their families to visit them. Their hopes rose as they shaved, washed, and were given clean shirts. Hour after hour he sat in his cell, but no one came. He did not know then that the postcards were never sent.

As night came, the loudspeakers began to blare: *Nobody loves you now . . . Nobody loves you now . . .* He began to weep. And then the loudspeaker said: *They don't want to know you any more . . . They don't want to know you any more . . .*

The next day he was told that plenty of other wives had come to visit. They told him he was a fool, that his wife was in bed with other men, and they described what was happening with all the obscenity they could. When he had enough of the lecture he was returned to his cell and over the loudspeaker came the chant: *Christianity is dead . . . Christianity is dead . . .*

He began to believe what they had told him all of those months, that Christianity was truly dead. He wrote,

> The Bible foretells a time of great apostasy, and I believed that it had arrived.
>
> Then I thought of Mary Magdalene, and perhaps this thought, more than any other, helped to save me from the soul-killing poison of the last and worst stage of brainwashing. I remembered how she was faithful to Christ even when He cried on the Cross, "My God, why have you forsaken me?" And when He was a corpse in the tomb, she wept nearby and waited until He arose. So when I believed at last that Christianity was dead, I said, "Even so, I believe in it, and I will weep at its tomb until it arises again, as it surely will."[3]

After he was released he wrote: "The prison years did not seem too long for me, for I discovered, alone in my cell, that beyond belief and love there is a delight in God: a deep and extraordinary ecstasy of happiness that is like nothing in this world."

Now the words written by that pastor twenty-three years ago have come true. Christianity has risen again in Rumania, and in many other countries in that part of the world. However, Christianity was never dead in those countries, for God was not dead in the hearts of believers. His love will never die.

"

His love for His children will never leave in times of trouble.

"

God is not blind. He knows about you and your problems. He knows of those who are suffering from the loss of a loved one, the knowledge of terminal illness, the memories of childhood abuse, the strain of financial failure, and your particular pain. And His love for His children will never leave in times of trouble.

Lew Wallace distinguished himself as a major general in the Union Army during the Civil War. He was a lawyer who served on the court-martial that tried the assassins of Abraham Lincoln, and he presided over the military court that convicted the superintendent of Andersonville Prison of cruelty in allowing the death of Union prisoners. Wallace was a strong, intelligent man, but he did not know the love of God. However, when he was challenged to read the Bible, to disprove the existence of God, instead, his heart was changed dramatically and he became a believer in Jesus Christ. Subsequently, he penned one of the best-sellers in Christian fiction, *Ben Hur*, which was made into one of the greatest films of all time, starring Charlton Heston.

Wallace, the tough war hero, wrote these words: "Riches take wings, comforts vanish, hope withers away, but love stays with us. God is love."

Before we can grasp any meaning from suffering, we must rest in His unfailing love.

3

Into Each Life Some Rain . . .

God is preparing His heroes and the time will come when they will appear and the world will wonder where they came from.
A. W. Tozer

IN MANY CASES, THE RAIN THAT FALLS is more like Hurricane Hugo of 1989. The winds of that tempest tore up the lives of thousands in its vicious path. Only in fairy tales do people live charmed lives. We may think that some people have it all, but if we turn the pages of their lives we may see the frog that never turned into a prince or the person who seemed "born to trouble."

Sometimes life touches one person with a bouquet and another with a thorn bush. But the first may find a wasp in the flowers, and the second may discover roses among the thorns.

Who Said Life Was Fair?

Have you ever heard a child wail, "It's not fair!" There are those who have made their fortunes on other people's misfortune. The Bible never promised that life would be fair. Christian living that sounds like an article on the lifestyle page of the newspaper may leave us unprepared for a world where hell does break loose. We are in a battle on this earth, and there is no one who is excused from service.

As we pray and give thanks for the end of the Berlin Wall and the opening of Eastern Europe to democracy and religious freedom, we also realize that new tyrannies challenge the Christian faith. We must not become complacent in our sanctuaries.

I met two Christians from an Eastern Bloc country who worked in a Christian radio station. When asked how it felt to be persecuted for their faith, they replied, "We thought it was the normal Christian life." They were right. It is we who are living abnormally—for the present.

The Popularity Cult

In some churches and religious television programs, we see an effort to make Christianity popular and always positive. This may be a comfortable cushion for those who find the hard facts too difficult. Within the New Testament, there is no indication that Christians should expect to be healthy, wealthy, and successful in this present age. Jesus said, "If the world hates you, keep in mind that it hated me first" (John 15:18). Christ never told his disciples that they would get an Academy Award for their performances, but He did tell them to expect to have troubles.

This age is interested in success, not suffering. We can identify with James and John who wanted choice seats in the kingdom. We might even ask for reclining chairs and soft music.

Our Lord was ridiculed, insulted, persecuted, and eventually killed. In the face of opposition, He went about "doing good." Even His enemies could find no fault in Him. He became the greatest teacher of moral values the world has ever known, but after only three years of public ministry He was executed as a criminal.

"Good" people do not escape suffering in this life. The Bible lists in Hebrews 11 the heroes of the faith, both Jew and Gentile, who were tortured, imprisoned, stoned, torn apart, and killed by the sword. They didn't wear designer jeans but went about in animal skins, destitute and tormented. Those early believers wandered in deserts, crossed mountains, and hid in caves. They were the homeless of that time, without even a cardboard shelter.

"

To be a disciple of Jesus means to learn from Him, to follow Him. The cost may be high.

"

In America today, being a Christian is sometimes equated with having good health. Some popular nutrition and psychology publications recommend that a sound body may require a strong spiritual life. Many of these writers lean toward a hybrid of Eastern religious thought and humanistic psychology, but others have been biblically sound. I believe that exercise and proper eating habits are very important, since the Bible says that the body is God's holy temple, but I don't think that superbodies equate with committed Christian discipleship. Some of the greatest saints I've known have been those with physical infirmities.

Joni Eareckson Tada is a living example. Joni cannot walk and has only limited use of her arms. God has used her to touch millions of lives as a result of her handicap. She is a greater testimony to His love than many others who have strong bodies. "For physical training is of some value, but godliness has value for all things" (1 Timothy 4:8).

The Cost of Discipleship

Discipleship is not limited to twelve first-century men. Webster says that a disciple is a pupil or follower of any teacher or school of religion. To be a disciple of Jesus means to learn from Him, to follow Him. The cost may be high.

In the earlier part of His ministry, great crowds followed Jesus. However, the moment He started telling His followers that they must take up their crosses, "many . . . no longer followed him" (John 6:66).

Many forms of suffering are predicted in the Bible. The list sounds like Foxes' *Book of Martyrs*: persecutions for righteousness, reviling and slander, false accusations, rejection, hatred by the world and by relatives, temptations, shame, imprisonments, stonings, beatings, being a public spectacle, and the list continues. Your personal pain may not relate to any of these, because it is unique to you and to your situation. It may not even be comforting to hear of these forms of punishment. In Western democracies, seldom have people been called to endure physical suffering because they were believers. However, there are many other types of suffering.

If you have ever lost your job because you refused to compromise your principles, you know the hurt. If a friend or family member has ever accused you of being a fanatic, you might have felt humiliated. If you're a teenager and your best friends have ever excluded you from a spring break beach party, the rejection may be very painful.

What about the average professing Christian? Is living for the Lord Jesus Christ a priority? Sadly, it may not be. In America, churchgoing has become popular, but attending a service (or a Crusade) may not necessarily be accompanied by genuine depth in prayer and Bible study or a change in the way we live.

Christianity is not a spectator sport, it's something in which we become totally involved. The Scripture says, "Therefore, if anyone is in Christ, he is a new creation; the old has gone, the new has come!" (2 Corinthians 5:17). Those who believe are expected to be different from the world about them. They are to be members of the new society and the new community that God has created.

"

Our job in life is not to be successful, but to be faithful.

"

Too many Christian television and radio programs have been geared to please, entertain, and gain the favor of this world. The temptation is to compromise, to make the Gospel more appealing and attractive.

At times in the Crusades we have conducted, I have looked into the cameras and realized that several million people were watching. I know that many of the things I have said from the Scriptures have offended some, but I cannot afford to tone down the message. As Paul said in 1 Corinthians 9:17, "I have a stewardship entrusted to me" (NASB), and that is to preach the pure and simple Gospel in whatever culture I am in.

The Bible says, "Don't let the world around you squeeze you into its own mold, but let God remold your minds from within" (Romans 12:2 PHILLIPS). Charles Colson wrote, "If Christianity is true—then it cannot be simply a file drawer in our crowded lives. It must be the central truth from which all our behavior, relationships, and philosophy flow."[1]

It is easy for Christians to allow themselves to be squeezed into the world's mold. It doesn't mean that we can't be fashionable, or that we have to wear drab clothing and live in hovels. It's the attitude of the world, rather than appearances, that we should not adopt. When nonbelievers see nothing different in the lifestyle of believers, they wonder if our profession of faith is sincere.

Our job in life is not to be successful, but to be faithful. Many Christians would prefer to hear "What a great guy" from the crowd rather than "Well done, good and faithful servant" from the Master.

Dietrich Bonhoeffer was a brilliant young German pastor from an aristocratic family of wealth and education. At the age of thirty-seven he was imprisoned by the Nazi government for his alleged involvement in an attempt to assassinate Hitler. He was never tried, but two years later, near the end of the war, Bonhoeffer was executed. Fellow prisoners who survived reported a message he sent to a friend, "Tell him that for me this is the end, but also the beginning." Bonhoeffer knew the cost of discipleship.

Many Christians want the benefits of their belief, but they hesitate at the cost of discipleship. Again, we have choices to make. Moses had a choice of following God or reveling in the pleasures of Egypt. As heir to the throne of Egypt, he enjoyed luxury; he didn't desire to suffer or sacrifice any more than we do, but he chose to follow God. "He chose to be mistreated along with the people of God rather than to enjoy the pleasures of sin for a short time" (Hebrews 11:25).

Salvation is free, but there is a price to pay in following Jesus. It is never said in Scripture that we can have "Christ and . . ."; it is always "Christ or . . ." Christ or Caesar, Christ or the world, Christ or Antichrist. What is your "or"?

Jesus said, "He who is not with me is against me, and he who does not gather with me scatters" (Matthew 12:30). Following Christ has been made too easy. It is easy to follow Him when our world is safe and comfortable, when we have good health, a contented family, and three meals (plus snacks) a day. But when that world shatters, only a secure faith will sustain us.

In a country where Christians were looked upon with suspicion and disfavor, a government leader said to me with a twinkle in his eye, "Christians seem to thrive under persecution. Perhaps we should prosper them, and then they would disappear."

"

Salvation is free,
but there is a price to pay
in following Jesus.

"

Gretchen's Story

Gretchen was a woman who had her comfortable world disintegrate in one blinding moment. Without her faith in God, she might have remained for the rest of her life hidden in a dark room.

As she told her story, she was sitting on a California patio, the brilliant sun emphasizing her cruelly disfigured face. It was obvious from the blank socket where one eye should have been, the reconstructed nose, the scarred skin, and the missing arm that she had been in some hideous accident. And yet her beauty was evident. The transcendent glow of her inner strength was not artificial.

Gretchen's world changed one morning in 1982 when a drunk driver forced her car into a fatal spin, hurtling it across the freeway, where it exploded into a burning inferno. Her mother was instantly killed, and Gretchen was miraculously saved from burning to death.

Before that dreadful day, Gretchen had led a sun-filled life. Beautiful, wealthy, with an attentive husband, she seemed to be living every girl's dream. In the following nightmare, she lost everything but gained much more.

She was in a coma for six weeks. When she finally understood that her face was virtually gone, she did not want anyone to see her. Television was her companion, and it was during one of her more than seventy operations that she saw one of our Crusades and gave her life to Christ.

After seven years of seclusion, she realized that she could not stay in hiding. She knew God had saved her for something. She began to volunteer at a rehabilitation center where her own disabilities gave her the credibility to reach out to others. When asked about her greatest joy, she answered, "It's waking up in the morning and knowing that nothing is an accident."

Cross-Bearers with Long Faces

The marks of the cross are not to be confused with self-inflicted austerity or the rigors of the Middle Ages brought up-to-date. We should not intentionally seek suffering with the mistaken idea that we might earn special merit with God. Asceticism is not necessarily a virtue.

Amy Carmichael wrote:

> The narrow thorny path he trod,
> 'Enter into my joy,' said God.
> The sad ascetic shaved his head,
> 'I've lost the taste for joy,' he said.

Christ admonished His followers: "When you fast, do not look somber as the hypocrites do, for they disfigure their faces to show men they are fasting" (Matthew 6:16). This was a clear warning not to boast of trials we have brought upon ourselves.

Bearing our cross does not mean wearing gunny sacks and long faces. Some people we meet imagine that every little headache is a part of their cross. They wear the look of a martyr every time they hear criticism. Sometimes we deserve the criticism we receive; however, we are blessed only when men speak evil against us *falsely* for Christ's sake.

> *"Christians should be a foreign influence, a minority group in a pagan world."*

A book was written about me that contained some blatant falsehoods. At first I was offended, but then I began to laugh, because I had just been talking about being blessed for false accusations and God gave me a personal illustration.

Christians should be a foreign influence, a minority group in a pagan world. We are the "light of the world," and light exposes evil. We are the salt, and it adds flavor. If we are at peace with this world, it may be because we have sold out to it and compromised with it.

Dwight L. Moody once said, "If the world has nothing to say against you, beware lest Jesus Christ has nothing to say for you."

Take Heart!

I am not suggesting that we live anticipating trouble at every turn. Some people spend so much time worrying about what might happen that they never enjoy what is happening. Take one day at a time. Today, after all, is the tomorrow you worried about yesterday.

Jesus knew His disciples were worried about the future, and when He talked to them at the end of His ministry, on the very eve of His death, He said, "I have told you these things, so that in me you may have peace. In this world you will have trouble. But take heart! I have overcome the world" (John 16:33).

Trouble is different for all of us—translate it as you will: money, marital, health, social, loneliness. Jesus said His followers would have trouble. But He also promises His presence with us, not to deliver us from our problems, but to be with us in the midst of them and give us the power to overcome whatever circumstances come our way.

Nancy Bates, one of our researchers, is an example of overcoming circumstances. She has a delightful sense of humor and is a joy to be around. Nancy was struck by a car when she was seventeen, and her back was broken. She is a paraplegic. And she is a contagious Christian.

When the Apostle John recorded Christ's message to the church in Smyrna, he wrote, "Do not be afraid of what you are about to suffer. I tell you, the devil will put some of you in prison to test you, and you will suffer persecution. . . . Be faithful, even to the point of death, and I will give you the crown of life" (Revelation 2:10).

Mysterious as it appears to be, true faith and suffering frequently go hand-in-hand. You seldom have one without the other. I think of my dear friend, Corrie ten Boom, who has gone home to be with the Lord. One incident in her last years comes to mind after reading the previous passage from Revelation.

After being a prisoner in Ravensbruk, the infamous women's concentration camp, Corrie traveled throughout the world, telling her story of suffering and joy. For thirty-three years she never had a permanent home. When she was eighty-five years old, her supporters provided her with a lovely house in California. It was a luxury she never dreamed she would have.

One day, as her friend and movie director, the late Jimmy Collier, was leaving her home, he said, "Corrie, hasn't God been good to give you this beautiful place?"

She replied firmly, "Jimmy, God was good when I was in Ravensbruk, too."

Suffering Is Not in Vain

No suffering that one of Christ's own endures for Him is ever in vain. Living for Christ, walking in His way, will not be an easy path. The way of the cross is a hard one, but He never said it would be easy.

> *The way of the cross is a hard one, but He never said it would be easy.*

The scriptural principles relating to the endurance of pain are just the same today as when they were first written for us in the Word of God. Some of us may have to die, or at least suffer, for our faith. The twentieth century has seen more people tortured and killed for Christ than any other century. Our generation has known its martyrs, like Paul Carlson, the missionary to the Congo who was killed trying to rescue others. Jim Elliot was killed, along with four friends, trying to get the Gospel to the Auca Indians in Ecuador. Bishop Luwum, the archbishop of the Anglican Church of Uganda, was shot in the head at point blank range.

Festo Kivengere was speaking in Asheville, North Carolina, and said this about Luwum's martyrdom: "When a man has lived for God, preaching the Gospel fearlessly, opposing cruelty, injustice, and oppression with courage, yet speaking the truth graciously and in love—when that man seals his testimony with his blood, that is not tragedy, that is glory!"

When Ruth was speaking in Sweden, her interpreter, Gunvar Paulson, told about being in the Salvation Army in Rhodesia when insurgents broke in and murdered many people. Her coworkers were killed. She alone was spared, but after repeated operations has only limited use of her left arm. Impulsively, Ruth said, "What an honor it is to sit beside you—I have never had to suffer for the Lord."

Miss Paulson replied, "Believe me, in spite of all that was going on around me, I felt such a sense of the presence of the Lord Jesus, it was pure joy!"

When David Livingstone returned to his native Scotland after sixteen difficult years as a missionary in Africa, his body was emaciated by the ravages of some twenty-seven fevers that had coursed through his veins during the years of his service. One arm hung useless at his side, the result of being mangled by a lion. He was speaking to the students at Glasgow University and the core of his message to those young people was this: "Shall I tell you what sustained me during the hardship and loneliness of my exile? It was Christ's promise, 'Lo, I am with you always, even unto the end.'"

That promise is ours as well.

4

Pain in Paradise

A recovery of the old sense of sin is essential to Christianity.

C. S. Lewis

WHERE DID PAIN BEGIN?

Could God have created a world without suffering?

Yes, He could, and He did.

In millenniums past there was a time when the universe and its undiscovered galaxies were in a state of complete harmony with their Maker. It was an existence beyond the comprehension of our finite minds; we cannot imagine a world that is older than we can even think and which existed without a hint of the suffering to come. However, into this Paradise came Satan, probably the most misunderstood person in the universe. Before Satan there was no sin, and before sin there was no pain.

Who is Satan? He is underestimated and frequently caricatured. Some think he is only a spiritual force, others have imagined him as a goblin or dismissed him as a myth. Today, however, when Satan worship is increasing at an alarming rate, we had better be aware of him, his origin, his aims, his abilities, and his limitations.

Satan was once a dazzling creature. The prophet Ezekiel called him "the model of perfection, full of wisdom and perfect in beauty" (28:12). This incredible person was once one of the "sons of God" (Job 38:7 NASB).

The First Sinner Commits the First Sin

Lucifer (meaning "morning star" in Hebrew) was an angel created to glorify God, but this was not the role he wanted. His heart's desire was to be the chief authority; he wanted to sit on God's throne and rule the universe. Isaiah 14:12–14 tells us: "How you have fallen from heaven, O morning star, son of the dawn! You have been cast down to the earth, you who once laid low the nations! You said in your heart, I will ascend to heaven; I will raise my throne above the stars of God; I will sit enthroned on the mount of assembly, on the utmost heights of the sacred mountain. I will ascend above the tops of the clouds; I will make myself like the Most High."

When Lucifer asserted his desire to be more than God, a great revolution took place in the universe. Many angels joined with Lucifer and became his rebel army. Evidently when God judged Lucifer's crimes, God changed his name to Satan, the Evil One, and sentenced him to eternal exile.

Satan didn't lose any of his beguiling ways when he became the fallen prince. He took his charm, his subtleties, and his clever plots to use on us. When he made his decision to battle God to the death, he took his band of rebel angels with him as his combat soldiers. The battlefield is known as Earth.

The Way It Was

Before the great polluter spread his poison throughout this new territory, God chose to beautify this planet with light and darkness, seas and skies, land and vegetation, sun, moon and stars, air, and land animals.

In a time when we are concerned about our polluted earth, can you imagine what Paradise was like? Every flower that grew was perfect; no blight was on them. The fertilizers and bug sprays we keep in our garden shed were not needed. Visualize a fruit tree laden with juicy apples or pears, without a bug in any piece. Imagine the sky so clear you could see every galaxy and constellation. No trash, no unpleasant odors, no litter. The lakes would have waters so clear you could see the color of every fish. God designed this glorious earth garden for His perfect children. When Adam and Eve were created they brought human beauty into this world of perfection.

The First Perfect Relationship

God wanted someone with whom He could fellowship. So He created Adam and Eve. No couple since then has had the ideal union that those two lovers had.

In the middle of the garden were two special trees, the *Tree of Life* and the *Tree of the Knowledge of Good and Evil.* The Lord God told the man, "You are free to eat from any tree in the garden; but you must not eat from the tree of the knowledge of good and evil, for when you eat of it you will surely die" (Genesis 2:16–17). Monsignor Knox translates it even more emphatically: "Thy doom is death!"

A river flowed out of Eden, dividing into four rivers, two of which were the Tigris and the Euphrates. So the Garden of Eden was somewhere in present-day Iraq. The turmoil and war we have recently witnessed in that part of the world in our time is occurring in the land where God established the first perfect civilization.

It became God's daily practice to walk with man in the garden in the cool of the day (Genesis 3:8). What an idyllic existence! How could anyone want more? And yet the first couple did.

God gave Adam and Eve more than beauty and a perfect environment. He gave them one of the most precious things man can have. Freedom. John Milton said, "When God gave Adam reason, he gave him freedom to choose . . . otherwise, he would have been a mere artificial Adam, such as an Adam in the puppet shows." Adam and Eve could have been created to walk where God directed them, speak the words God gave them—just mere puppets. However, God gave them, just as He has given us, freedom to choose.

Satan's Tactics

Satan entered the garden in the form of a serpent. We can only speculate how this happened, but we do know that he had been on the prowl, searching for ways to destroy God ever since the time of his banishment from Heaven. And here was his opportunity to hurt two who were dear to the heart of God. He started in the same subtle way he uses today.

He cast doubt on what God had said. He worked on Eve first when he said, "Did God really say . . . ?" (Genesis 3:1). The next strategy Satan used was an appeal to the ego. He told Eve she wouldn't die when she ate of that certain tree, she would simply be like God. So Eve took the fatal bite and passed some over to Adam, and he ate. This is called the Fall of man, and it has been a long way down ever since. God said to Adam, "Have you eaten from the tree that I commanded you not to eat from?" (Genesis 3:11). Adam answered by saying, "The woman *you* put here with me—she gave me some fruit from the tree, and I ate it" (Genesis 3:12, emphasis added).

Ever since, man has been passing the blame. A boy sins, his parents are blamed. A person is murdered, his environment is blamed. Someone cheats, the system is blamed. Passing the blame is as old as the Garden of Eden.

Even worse, man keeps asking, *How can a just and loving God allow so much suffering in the world—natural disasters—man's inhumanity to man?* Somehow, like Adam, man tries to blame God.

Beginning of Sorrow

Human nature was now flawed. Man's direct disobedience resulted in the judgment God placed on the human race.

The beginning of all pain and suffering in the world started with one act of disobedience. Christian and non-Christian alike have inherited the consequences from our common ancestors, Adam and Eve—our polluted environment and flawed human nature.

What Is This Thing Called Sin?

Satan exalted himself above God and endeavored to get man to doubt the reliability of God's Word. If Adam and Eve had resisted the devil, he would have fled, defeated. But they didn't (Genesis 3:13). This is where death began! A three-dimensional death:

1. Instant spiritual death: separation from God.
2. Gradual physical death: as soon as we are born we begin to die.
3. Ultimate eternal death—but for the saving mercy of Jesus Christ.

Sin works the same with all of us, whatever our condition, nature, or environment. We are depraved by nature because we inherited it (Romans 3:19), and we must bear the sentence of guilt and the stain of sin. Each person must give an account of himself to God.

One Crisis After Another

One crisis has followed another throughout human history—Cain murdered Abel—the Flood came and only Noah and those in the Ark were saved—confusion fell upon Babel as different languages were introduced—and so on, down through history until today.

Confusion of Good and Evil

We have seen the progression of the "father of lies." He began in Eden. He was behind each of the major crises of faith and obedience down through the centuries. And he still deceives gullible men and women of every age.

> "*Man's direct disobedience resulted in the judgment God placed on the human race.*"

An old Scottish clergyman said the devil has two lies that he uses at two different stages. Before we commit a sin, he tells us that one little sin doesn't matter—"no one will know." The second lie is that after we've sinned he tells us we're hopeless. We have all fallen, individually and collectively, and God does not consider this a trifling matter. Judgment hangs over the whole human race because of rebellion and disobedience. The Scripture says, "Sin entered the world through one man, and death through sin, and in this way death came to all men, because all sinned" (Romans 5:12).

The good news is because Jesus Christ came and died on the cross and rose from the dead, we are not in a hopeless position. We can be reconciled to God and put back in right relationship with Him by accepting His provision for sin, His Son Jesus Christ.

As sin has progressed and gained momentum, modern man seems to have lost his ability to be shocked. Behavior that was once considered abominable is now acceptable. One thing is certain, however. There are many new sinners today, but there aren't any new sins, just the old ones clothed in different rags.

Sin invariably hurts the innocent—frequently worse than it does the one committing it.

I have found, however, that most young people really want us to spell out a moral code. They may not accept it or believe it, but they want to hear it, clearly and without compromise. But where can the moral code be found?

The state highway department in Pennsylvania once set out to build a bridge, working from both sides. When the workers reached the middle of the waterway, they found they were thirteen feet to one side of each other. Albert Steinberg, writing some time ago in the *Saturday Evening Post,* went on to explain that each crew of workmen had used its own reference point.

There's a small disc on the Meades Ranch in north central Kansas where the thirty-ninth parallel from the Atlantic to the Pacific crosses the ninety-eighth meridian running from Canada to the Rio Grande. The National Oceanic Survey, a small federal agency whose business it is to locate the exact positions of every point in the United States, uses the scientifically recognized reference point on the Meades Ranch. So far, no mistakes have been made, and none are expected.

All ocean liners and commercial planes come under the survey. The government can build no dams or even launch a missile without this agency to tell it the exact location to the very inch. "Location by approximation," the article goes on to say, "can be costly and dangerous."

In the field of surveying, the word *benchmark* is of ultimate significance. It is the point of reference from which a surveyor takes all his measurements. If the benchmark is wrong, all of his calculations will be wrong. Where you start will determine where you end.

The same thing is true about the compass, the sextant, and the sun and the stars. If the compass is not accurate, you will lose your way. If the sun and the stars were not ordered in their stations, no mariner could depend on them to find his way through the oceans of the world. If there are no absolutes, no fixed reference points, there can be no certainty. The locus of the conflict in the world today rises from the battle between the absolute and the relative.

The reference point from which I approach you today is that of a Christian who believes in the Bible. All my values, judgments, and attitudes must be gauged in relationship to this reference point. If you are coming from another reference point, then you and I may have a very difficult time meeting.

Pain in Paradise: Suffering at Home

Why do we suffer? Why does life seem so unfair, so unjust? One thing is clear. The Bible explains that there is suffering in the world because there is sin in the world. The root of the problem lies in man's alienation from God which began with Adam and Eve. If the separation that sin creates had not entered into the life of man, human suffering would not exist in the world.

In God's original blueprint, suffering was not drawn in the plans. By willful disobedience to God's Word and commandment, man brought suffering upon himself. He has been reaping what he has sown all through the centuries. And he blames God. Repeatedly. Daily. "How could a loving God allow . . . ?" "How can God be just and permit . . . ?" It is always God's fault.

Is it really necessary to know how suffering entered the world? I believe that we need to know the origin of pain, or we would be like the physician prescribing medicine without an examination.

"

The locus of the conflict
in the world today
rises from the battle between
the absolute and the relative.

"

God does not offer Band-Aids when you are bleeding to death, but He gave a life-saving transfusion, the blood of His Son. God is not responsible for sin, but His love led Him to send His Son to die for our sins.

> Look, Father, look on His beloved face
> And only look on us as seen in Him.
> Look not on our misusing of Thy grace
> Our prayer so languid and our faith so dim
> For, lo, between our sins and their reward,
> We place the passion of Thy Son, our Lord.

5

Why Jesus Suffered

When I consider my crosses, tribulations, and temptations, I shame myself almost to death, thinking what are they in comparison to the suffering of my blessed Savior Christ Jesus.

Martin Luther

A GRANDMOTHER IS WATCHING HER small grandson when the phone rings. She talks for a few minutes while he climbs the fence and drowns in the pool.

Three high school athletes are hit and killed by a drunk driver.

A beautiful teenager is reported missing. Her distraught parents find her on the streets of San Francisco, living as a prostitute.

Your minister's child is diagnosed with incurable cancer.

Your son is held as a hostage in a foreign land.

Friday comes, and along with your paycheck is a termination notice.

These are anguishing scenarios of human suffering. Perhaps you may have had some heart-breaking times of your own that are worse than these. When we go through some of life's hard trials, it is natural to center upon ourselves. Whether it is physical or mental anguish, personal pain tears us apart.

God did not exclude Himself from human suffering. He became man—the Person of Christ—and shared with us all there is to share. Philip Yancey wrote, "God does not, in the comfortable surroundings of heaven, turn a deaf ear to the sounds of suffering on this groaning planet."[1]

God Joined Us

We have read stories, seen many paintings, and sat through numerous Christmas pageants about the birth of Jesus. It never ceases to stir me.

Jesus life was in peril from the time He uttered His first cry. The most illustrious child ever born was hated by many while He lay in a manger, helpless to defend Himself.

We don't know much about His life as a child, but we do know that He lived with the knowledge of His destiny. His entire life was one of humiliation; He came not as a conquering king, which is what the Jews expected, but as a humble servant.

When He was an adult, the leaders were suspicious of this carpenter from Nazareth, because He was a threat to them. They scorned Him and treated Him with contempt. They said He broke God's law, that He was an unholy person—a drunkard and one who made friends with the scum of society. He had the label of guilt by association stamped upon Him by self-righteous men.

Many people reacted to Him violently. At the beginning of His ministry, His own townsfolk at Nazareth tried to throw Him off a cliff (Luke 4:29). Religious and political leaders often conspired to seize and kill Him. And yet He healed the sick, fed the hungry, loved the unlovely, taught the ignorant, and worked miracles among His people. Ultimately, He was arrested and brought to trial before Pilate and Herod. Though innocent, He was denounced as an enemy of God and man. The frenzied mob incited the religious leaders and cried, "Crucify Him!"

Remember, too, that He knew in advance what was coming, and this increased His suffering. He knew the path of pain He would experience; He foresaw the baptism of blood that awaited Him. He told His disciples very plainly about His coming death by crucifixion, which they could not understand at the time.

The Cross: Symbol of Suffering

Jesus suffered more than any other person in human history. The specifics of how He suffered were predicted in the prophecies of the Old Testament some five hundred to a thousand years before these events occurred.

When we are in trouble, we need a friend. We need someone to understand, to be with us, to hold us close and say, "I'm here to help." When Jesus needed friends, they left Him.

What a devastation! At the end of training the twelve, they failed Him miserably. Anyone who has been deserted knows the terrible feeling of abandonment. Jesus had to appear alone before His accusers. He had to face His trial without a friend.

"

Jesus suffered more than any other person in human history.

"

When Jesus was arrested, it was a religious lynching. False witnesses accused Him, "looking for false evidence against Jesus so that they could put him to death. But they did not find any" (Matthew 26:59–60).

The Jewish authorities were determined to have Him killed, but they needed to get the permission of Pilate, the man appointed by Rome to be in charge of Jerusalem. Jews, under Roman rule, did not have the right to carry out the death penalty. Pilate was convinced that Jesus was not guilty; three times he pronounced Him innocent. Then he had an idea he thought would absolve him of making a decision. It was his custom to release one prisoner at the time of Passover. "'Do you want me to release the "king of the Jews"?' They shouted back, 'No, not him! Give us Barabbas!'" (John 18:39–40.)

Pilate was disappointed when the crowd chose Barabbas, a common criminal, instead of Jesus. He must have cringed when he led the pitiful, bruised, and bleeding man before the crowd. Instead of sympathy, he heard the shouts, "Crucify! Crucify!"

Pilate was a weak man, and when the chief priests told him that he would be Caesar's enemy if he did not kill this revolutionary, he gave in. Before he handed Jesus over to be crucified, he called for a basin and said, "I am innocent of this man's blood. It is your responsibility." He washed his hands of the whole affair.

All Signs Point to the Cross

The cross of Jesus Christ was the culmination of the one life that held more suffering than any other in human history. His was the suffering of the entire world. And God made Him who had no sin to be sin for us (2 Corinthians 5:21). Since the day of crucifixion, the cross has been the supreme symbol of salvation from sin.

God says there is no hope for the world aside from the cross. We look to the leadership of men, the progress of scientific discovery, or the spread of knowledge and think human beings can find solutions to our problems. But our hope rests not in a system, or a government, or a philosophy, but in the cross of Christ.

To many people, the mention of the blood of Christ is distasteful. However, on my last visit to the Mayo clinic I noticed that at each reception desk there is a box holding large square pamphlets entitled *A Gift of Life* urging people to donate blood to the blood bank. Anyone who has gone through surgery and looked up to see the bag of blood dripping slowly into his veins, realizes with gratitude the life-giving property of blood.

The message of the blood, the cross, and the work of redemption is still "foolishness" to those who are perishing (1 Corinthians 1:18), but "to us who are being saved, it is the power of God."

Is God on Trial?

In past generations it was thought that mankind was on trial before a holy God. Now it seems that the reverse is true; people imagine God on trial for all the terrible things that happen. At the beginning of this chapter we cited some painful illustrations of real people undergoing real suffering. It is human to question, "Where is God when . . . ?" And you can finish the sentence with your own cry.

> "*God says there is no hope for the world aside from the cross.*"

When Jesus Christ was on the cross, His blood draining the life from His body, He knew what it was like to be alone, questioning God when He was wracked with pain. But His pain was the suffering of the sins of the ages, the greatest darkness of the soul ever known to man.

Why did Jesus suffer? For you. For me. That we might have life eternal and His peace in the midst of storms. "Peace I leave with you; my peace I give you. I do not give to you as the world gives. Do not let your hearts be troubled and do not be afraid" (John 14:27).

Suffering has no meaning unless we can believe that God understands our pain and can heal it. In the suffering of Jesus we have that assurance.

6

Who Sinned?

Few love to hear the sins they love to act.
William Shakespeare

SOME PEOPLE SEE SIN IN EVERY SICKNESS. They make their friends miserable by probing for hidden sins whenever suffering enters their lives. Although there may be some truth in their questioning, it also could be a cruel response to another's time of pain. They are like Job's so-called friends who pointed out all of his wrongs. Job called them "miserable comforters."

A child was dying of leukemia, and all hope had been abandoned. Her parents received a call from a woman who said she was a "healer." Grasping for any way to help their daughter or prolong her life, they asked the woman to come to their home. When she arrived, she asked a few questions, looked briefly at the weak, bedridden child, and then pronounced, "There's something wrong here. I detect sin in this house." The little girl heard these words and began to cry, "Make her leave, make her leave."

It is unkind to attribute every accident, every illness and sorrow to God's punishment for wrong behavior. It is appalling how many Christians approach suffering friends with that principle. They visit first with words of comfort, and then leave a load of guilt behind ("What could you have done to deserve this?") or pious advice ("Perhaps you need to pray harder.").

Suffering people can be tormented with questions of guilt; however, if all suffering is punishment for sin, then God's signals must be mixed, for accidents occur at random and disease strikes without any relationship to a person's moral or immoral lifestyle.

God's teaching does not attribute all suffering to sin or punishment for human mistakes. I have no right to tell a suffering person that it is because he sinned that his child died, or that he has cancer, or that his house burned.

In John 9, the followers of Jesus pointed to a man born blind and asked, "Who sinned, this man or his parents?" Jesus told them that neither the man nor his parents sinned, "But this happened so that the work of God might be displayed in his life." The disciples wanted to look back, to probe into the behavior of the blind man or his parents, but Jesus pointed them to the future and the hope that even suffering can be used to glorify God.

Who Needs Job's Friends?

Job was one man who endured such incredible suffering that most of us would say, "Don't tell me about Job; I could never relate to him." But in Job's story God has given us great examples of the type of questions or advice well-meaning friends sometimes express. (Is God trying to tell you something, Job? There must be a cause for your suffering. Is there some sin in your life? Repent, Job, that's the way out of your misery.)

Job had his world collapse around him. All of his possessions were wiped out, his seven sons and three daughters were killed in a tornado, and he was inflicted with painful, oozing boils from the top of his head to the bottom of his feet. What did he do to deserve these calamities? It was written that he was a man who was "blameless, upright, fearing God, and turning away from evil."

Yet Satan had to get permission from God before he could touch Job's possessions, much less Job himself. Somehow, all of the reasons for Job's suffering that his friends pointed out to him sound like those offered by Christians today. At one point, Job cried out to the men who berated him with his sins, "If it is true that I have gone astray, my error remains my concern alone" (Job 19:4).

One writer said, "Job is finally satisfied not by having his questions answered, but by a revelation of the incomparable majesty of God."[1] In the end, it was Job's friends who had their self-righteous theories dismissed. God said to Elephaz, one of the friends, "I am angry with you and your two friends, because you have not spoken of me what is right, as my servant Job has" (Job 42:7).

Philip Yancey wrote: "The Book of Job should nail a coffin lid over the idea that every time we suffer it's because God is punishing us or trying to tell us something. Although the Bible supports the general principle that 'a man reaps what he sows' even in this life (see Psalms 1:3; 37:25), the Book of Job proves that other people have no right to apply that general principle to a particular person. Nobody deserved suffering less than Job, and yet few have suffered more."[2]

The Book of Job does not set out to answer the problem of suffering, but to proclaim a God so great that no answer is needed.

Mistaken Thinking About Suffering

Among God's most obnoxious children are those who attribute all suffering to sin or punishment for mistakes. However, there's another error in thinking, and that is to assume that once we come to Christ, it will be almost impossible for sin to dominate us again. We may believe this because the Bible says, "If anyone is in Christ, he is a new creation; the old has gone, the new has come!" (2 Corinthians 5:17).

We think we're OK because our tempers have improved, our souls are calmer, our worldly desires have dwindled. *I'm OK no matter what trials and suffering hit me. I'm ready for them!*

The Trials Come

God's proving ground comes when trouble hits and the evil motives in our lives begin to surface. When you're on a lake where the water is calm and clear, the rainbow ripples of light playing on the surface, everything has an air of peace and beauty. But let the winds rise and the clouds open, and the water churns, bringing up the dredges of dirt and muck from the bottom. So it is with our lives. When calamity hits us, hard thoughts of God may begin to surface. *If God is so loving and wise, why did He allow this to happen?*

Archbishop Leighton said, "Extraordinary afflictions are not always the punishment of extraordinary sins, but sometimes the trial of extraordinary graces. God hath many sharp-cutting instruments and rough files for the polishing of His jewels; and those He especially loves, and means to make the most resplendent, He hath oftenest His tools upon."

Are we immune from evil thoughts and depraved actions when confronted with trials? Even some saints of old, when tried in God's proving grounds, were found not only evil, but many times their depravity was the last we would expect.

King David took one look at Bathsheba, another man's wife, and went after her. When Bathsheba became pregnant, David arranged to have her husband killed. When Peter faced guilt by association, he denied that he knew Jesus. All through the Bible we find occasional illustrations of strong men of old, believing in God, but revealing their innermost evil thoughts and actions in the face of trials.

God Tells Us Our Faults

We are told, "My son, do not make light of the Lord's discipline, and do not lose heart when he rebukes you" (Hebrews 12:5). What does it mean to be rebuked? It's the same word that is used in other passages to indicate that God "tells us our faults." He may begin His rebuke very gently. Simply read what He says to the churches in the Book of Revelation. With most of them He mentions past services and good deeds, but then comes the rebuke. "Yet I hold this against you: You have forsaken your first love," He told the angel of the church in Ephesus.

How do we know when we are being rebuked by God? Some rebukes are light and others are heavier, but when they are light (like the paddle ending in a soft cushion labeled "Grandma's paddle" which hangs in our front hall and has been given as a joke to many doting grandmothers), we tend to pay little attention.

> "*God's proving ground comes when trouble hits and the evil motives in our lives begin to surface.*"

Have you noticed when people tell us our faults, we can become discouraged? But when God points them out, we are not discouraged. With His rebuke comes the longing to do better. It may be that God is whispering to us with some light trial. That "still small voice" may be a warning, a tugging at our conscience.

Stronger Medicine

Can the sin of one or a few cause suffering for many? The answer, of course, is yes, for no sin is isolated in the life of the sinner. It spreads like poison gas into every available crevice. What may have been the rebellion against God of a few men has resulted in the most insidious plague the world has known. The influence of sin touches the innocent as well as the guilty . . . perhaps more.

From the sexually freewheeling culture of the sixties and seventies we inherited the AIDS epidemic. In the early years of its discovery, the response from the Christian community ranged from panic to self-righteousness, mostly wrapped in ignorance.

The Bible clearly teaches that practicing homosexuality is a sin, but to classify AIDS as simply a homosexual disease would be a disastrous public policy. Former Surgeon General C. Everett Koop estimates that by the end of 1991 as many as 270,000 cases of AIDS will have occurred and, in the United States alone, 179,000 people will have died since the disease was reported ten years ago. Because of their sexual practices, homosexual men are efficient transmitters of AIDS, and they make up between 60 and 75 percent of the reported cases. However, one quarter of the cases are intravenous drug users, and one out of every ten victims got the virus through heterosexual sex or blood transfusion. And many are born with AIDS through an infected mother, or through some as yet unidentified way.

If AIDS had never become a disease, practicing homosexuality would still be wrong, according to the Bible. The problems of sexual relations outside of our marriage vows that have caused grief and disease and brokenness would still exist. Our sins catch up with us, and they magnify our capacity to cause suffering.

> *"The influence of sin touches the innocent as well as the guilty."*

I believe that many AIDS victims have been graciously given time. When they learn of the seriousness of their affliction, they have a chance to realize the love of God and His grace. The church should be ministering to these people and extending to them the promise of His forgiveness.

Sex: Sin and Not Sin

Some say that the sexual revolution is slowing down. People are seeing the ravages of AIDS and adjusting their lifestyles. Charles Colson said, "There is painful irony in the fact that it took AIDS to accomplish what no amount of pulpit pounding could do. People have a greater fear of disease than of God's judgment!"[3]

A loving God ordained monogamous marriage and the sanctity of what we call the traditional family. Within the bounds of marriage, sex is a gift of God, but when it is misused the possibilities are frightening. This is nothing new in our generation. Sexual immorality has always been a cause of death, judgment, and Hell. AIDS has clearly reminded our society of that, but the reality is not limited to AIDS.

Fatal Attraction, a popular movie of recent years, told the story of a supposedly respectable man who decided one short affair outside his marriage wouldn't hurt. The beautiful woman with whom he slept turned out to be a borderline psychotic who then crosses the border. In the film's terrifying climax, she nearly kills his wife. The story reflects what deep within our hearts we already know; if we want our lives to be good, indulging in what is unholy is risky business, to put it mildly.

The gift of sex is misused with reckless disregard for the consequences. Tragically, within the Christian ministry we see occasional examples of that abuse. What was meant by God to be beautiful within the bounds of marriage is degraded in everything from advertisements for perfume to comic strips. How much further, oh God, can it go?

The Bible shows Jesus dealing with sexual sin in several stories. The woman described in John 8 is one. Jesus had been praying all night before this event took place. He was teaching on the porch of the Temple, and a crowd had gathered. Suddenly there was a rude interruption as the Pharisees dragged before Him a poor woman who had been taken in immorality. She was crying. She expected to be stoned. It was a setup to trap Jesus by asking Him what should be done with the woman.

Jesus' dilemma was this: If He said yes to stone her, He would be in trouble with the Roman authorities, because they alone held the power of capital punishment. If He said not to stone her, He would break the law of Moses. He would be caught either way. So Jesus stooped down and wrote something on the ground. We can only guess what He wrote in the sand that day. Could it have been that He wrote the Ten Commandments?

He said, "If any one of you is without sin, let him be the first to throw a stone at her" (John 8:7). Imagine those religious leaders shifting from one foot to another, their eyes on the ground, not daring to look at one another. None of them could cast the first stone, because they were all guilty. They had dragged themselves to judgment, just as they had dragged the woman. Unfortunately, some Christians have treated those with AIDS in the same way, trying to make a point in an argument, instead of seeing the victim as one more of us sinners needing to be forgiven and cared for.

We understand this story, because we know we are, in our own way, standing in the crowd needing forgiveness, too. We may not be guilty of adultery, but we may be guilty of idolatry, lust, greed, or whatever our private or personal sin is. We may not carry the AIDS virus ourselves, but God forbid as modern-day Pharisees we should condemn others while carrying the virus of our own unconfessed and unrepented sins.

When Sigmund Freud began writing in the early part of this century, he complained of the narrowness of the Victorian era and attributed many neuroses to the sexual repression of his society. But if Freud were to come back today, he might reverse his stand and attribute our modern mania to the license and lack of sexual boundaries.

Historically the church, for the most part, has tried to teach that guilt and suffering are a result of sexual immorality. That is why there is no such thing as "safe sex." It may be sterile and clinically free of disease, but it is not safe from the pain of heartbreak it may cause. However, what right does any church have even attempting to approve of lifestyles or certain acts for which God prescribed the death penalty in the Old Testament?

Why did God make us sexual beings? I was speaking to the cadets at West Point, and as we were driving away, the chaplain said to me, "You know, God gave us one of the most difficult things ever to handle . . . sex." He asked me if I knew why. I said I thought I did. In the first place, God has given us sex to attract us to the opposite sex. That is natural and normal. In the very beginning, He looked at all He had made and called it good.

Second, sex was given for the propagation of the race. None of us would be here if it weren't for sex. That is the way God intended it, and it is the way He meant, within the bonds of matrimony, to produce children.

God has given us our sexuality as a means of expressing our love. This is why sex is not just for playboys to amuse themselves; it is the deepest way we can say to our spouse, "I love you and only you. I give myself completely to you alone."

Human sexuality was given as a glorious contribution to married love. It was given so that a man and a woman could express the unity that binds them together. We find ourselves in emotional quicksand if we go outside those rules of marriage, frequently resulting in depression, despair, or possibly disease.

"Human sexuality was given as a glorious contribution to married love."

Sin has a great impact on sex. It follows that if sin affects your sex life, it will also affect the rest of your life. Often it drives people to seek refuge in further sexual activities and other diversions, instead of turning to God.

Rebels against God who have misused the gift of their human sexuality are a growing army during our day. What God has given us as a gift of joy has often been turned into an instrument for our own destruction. But there is the wonderful good news of God's compassion, like that of Jesus speaking to the woman who was dragged before Him for her adulterous acts. Jesus told her to leave her life of sin and that she would not be condemned.

Rebels against God come in many forms. Some believe every disease, every accident, is caused by sin. Their judgmental attitude causes heartache in many lives. Other rebels defy God's laws and cause pain for themselves that may multiply in the lives of others.

Pious and judgmental attitudes will not soothe troubled hearts. The hope is in Jesus Christ, the light sent into this hopeless world.

7

Why God's Children Suffer

The explosion of Jesus upon one's life transforms the human personality. It often brings peace of mind, contentment, happiness and joy. But to stop there as many do is like comparing real life to a children's fairy tale in which the heroes and heroines "live happily ever after."
Charles Colson, *Life Sentence*

A NEW BELIEVER IN JESUS MAY RECEIVE false impressions of the normal Christian life. He may hear a preacher who wants to win his hearers to Christ and therefore glamorizes the Christian experience by making it sound as carefree and positive as he can. Many times believers begin their Christian walk on an emotional high. They see remarkable answers to prayer and experience the world in a rosy glow.

I cannot help comparing this feeling to that of the American public during the first few days of the war in the Persian Gulf. Everything seemed to be going our way as our brave pilots crushed enemy installations with little opposition. However, President George Bush, in a television talk, warned against "euphoria" as a result of these apparent successes.

Marine training is extremely tough. The physical discipline they experience is more than most of them have ever had. Even the most physically fit are left exhausted. In addition, the mental discipline drives them to the limit of their abilities. In actual combat, all of this training is put to use. How much more dangerous it would have been if they were given easy tasks during their training and praised for every accomplishment.

Being a Christian does not exempt us from tough training, which may mean suffering. If the training were easy, we would not be prepared for the tough days ahead.

Tactical Errors

There are two great errors we may make in our response to suffering. The first error is in thinking that the teacher is cruel. Many marines think that about their drill sergeants, until they go into combat.

The second error is to be prepared but to deny the possibility that we might be wounded or captured. The Christian life is a battlefield. The antithesis is the wealth-and-health theology, which says that we deserve God's material and physical blessings just because we are one of His children. If we fall into either of these two errors in our thinking, we will continually be anguished over the question of why Christians suffer.

I cannot answer why an innocent child dies after a lingering illness, nor why a great minister's life is cut short when his fruitful ministry is so desperately needed. As I write this book, one of my friends is dying of cancer, another had a heart attack, another a brain tumor, and another a stroke.

I do not believe mere suffering teaches us. If that were so the whole world would be wise! However, I do know the Bible shows us some valid reasons that may answer the scoffers who say, "If your God is so great, why doesn't He save you from your pain?"

Because We Are Human

When we are children we hear that goodness has its reward and badness has its punishment. If you're good, you get ice cream; if you're bad, you go to bed early. This can develop into a mushy theological teaching that if you work in the church, attend Bible studies, and support noble causes, you will somehow be rewarded. When rough times come, the victims may think, "After all I've done for the Lord, why is He putting me through this?" We bargain with the Lord, exchanging our good deeds for His blessings. We revert to childish thinking about gold stars on the chart for good behavior.

At the end of the Gulf War I went to Greensburg, Pennsylvania, to speak at a memorial service for those who had been killed in their barracks in Dhahran by a Scud missile. A small area of Pennsylvania lost about one-fourth of all the casualties that we had in that war. The people were asking me, "Why would God allow it?" Disasters, troubles, and illnesses are the common lot of mankind, and Christians and non-Christians are involved in them because we share the human experience.

Because We Sin or Disobey God

If a Christian loses his temper, tells a lie, or commits a sin of any kind, he will suffer God's chastisement or judgment. The Apostle Peter told the believers of his day that judgment must begin first among God's own children (see 1 Peter 4:17). Just as a child needs correcting, so God's children need correcting.

Many children today are growing up without discipline. As they become adults and the discipline of job or family demands are placed upon them, they do not know how to cope. Today's children need discipline to be useful members of society. Likewise, God's children need discipline to be useful members of His family.

The Scripture says the Lord disciplines those He loves, and He punishes everyone He accepts as a son. "Endure hardship as discipline: God is treating you as sons. For what son is not disciplined by his father? . . . No discipline seems pleasant at the time, but painful. Later on, however, it produces a harvest of righteousness and peace for those who have been trained by it" (Hebrews 12:7, 11).

A Christian has tremendous responsibilities to his own family. Husbands and wives are to love each other and to submit to one another. We are to train our children in the way in which they *should* go, not the way they *would* go. My wife and her wonderful parents trained our children as they were growing up, during the difficult times when I was gone so much. God blessed me with a woman who knew how to discipline with love.

If we neglect the responsibilities within our own families, we will suffer the consequences. Perhaps not immediately, but later.

I know of a Christian leader who had been unkind to his wife for years, until she suffered a complete physical and mental breakdown. He became infatuated with his secretary, but he wanted to remain a leader in his community. He wanted it all, but he could not have it all. He suffered a terrible battle within himself until the smile was gone from his face and joy had left his heart. His situation became so obvious that others learned of his circumstances and exposed his sin. His suffering became unbearable, all because of his own sin. As far as I know, he has not yet repented.

If we are unloving or unfaithful in our Christian life, we will pay for it with a guilty conscience or chastisement from God. Many Christians who profess Christ do not live as though they possess Him. There are hypocrites in the church, even in the pulpit and teaching in Bible schools and seminaries. The nonbeliever looks at them and says, "If that's what Christianity is all about, count me out." However, there were hypocrites in Jesus' day, too. He was not gentle with them. He said, "Woe to you . . . you hypocrites! You shut the kingdom of heaven in men's faces" (Matthew 23:13).

To Discipline Us

My brother Melvin tried to describe what I was like as a boy and said that we didn't then know the term "hyper," but if we had, that is what he would have called me. I guess you might say that I crackled with nervous energy. In fact, one of my teachers told my mother, "Billy will never amount to anything."

So I had my share of discipline. My father was not one to spare the rod. However, there is one thing I knew in my heart. My father loved me.

> *"God's children need discipline to be useful members of His family."*

Jesus says, "Those whom I love I rebuke and discipline" (Revelation 3:19). God's discipline is one of love. The life of a Christian may be hard, but God has His divine plan for shaping our lives, and that plan often includes suffering.

I remember visiting Dohnavur, India, which was the home of a remarkable woman. She had written more than forty books. And she spent the last twenty years of her life as a bedridden invalid, but it was during that time that she did most of her writing. That woman was Amy Carmichael.

As I stood in the simple room that had been her personal prison for all that time, the presence of Christ was so very real to me that when I was asked to lead in prayer, I broke down and could not continue. Turning to my traveling companion, the great German industrialist, John Bolton, a very disciplined and apparently unemotional man, I said, "John, you pray." He began, but after a few words he, too, broke down, unable to continue, the tears streaming down his handsome face.

When I talk about suffering, which includes all the elements of pain and anguish known to man, not just physical pain, I'm no different from you. I would like to lead a life free of problems, free of pain, and free of severe personal discipline. However, I have had extreme pressures in my life to the point where I have wanted to run away from reality. I have even been tempted to ask the Lord to take me to Heaven.

C. S. Lewis said in *The Problem of Pain,* "You would like to know how I behave when I am experiencing pain, not writing books about it. You need not guess, for I will tell you; I am a great coward. . . . But what is the good of telling you about my feelings? You know them already; they are the same as yours. I am not arguing that pain is not painful. Pain hurts."[1]

I must admit I feel very inadequate at times when talking about God's discipline through pain. I have been close to those who have lost their children in accidents or lingering illnesses. My own nephew, Sandy Ford, a campus leader at the University of North Carolina, died after an operation for a rare heart disorder. I was with Leighton and Jean in their hour of suffering.

I have been with leaders whose careers were ruined by their own bad choices. I have been in areas devastated by earthquakes, fires, and bombs. When those I love have suffered, I have wished I could take their pain as my own. However, I have lived past the three score and ten, and my wife, my children, grandchildren, and great-grandchildren are all living. How dare I speak of the discipline of suffering? Without God's Word and examples from the lives of believers, I would be as inadequate to write about suffering as a child would be to explain nuclear physics.

God's discipline is one of wisdom. Horatius Bonar says, "What deep wisdom then must there be in all His dealings!

He knows exactly what we need and how to supply it. . . . The time and the way and the instrument are all according to the perfect wisdom of God."[2]

"

The rewards of some may even be greater in the future life because they suffered when there was no relief in sight.

"

When Charles Colson was sent to prison for his participation in the Watergate scandal, it was the wisdom of God that utilized his sentence. A judge may have been the human instrument through whom God worked, but the result was God's plan for the life of a man who has since ministered to thousands inside and outside of prisons around the world.

The wisdom of God's discipline may be obscured when we are in the midst of suffering. In the Faith Chapter in the Bible (Hebrews 11) there is a list of some of God's great heroes. Noah, Abraham, Isaac, Jacob, Joseph, and Moses were some of those old believers. Many were gloriously delivered because of their faith. But others were tortured, flogged, stoned, imprisoned, and lost all their possessions.

In this great roll call of faith, beginning with the second half of verse 35, we have God's "Medal of Honor" list. The last two verses of Hebrews 11 tell us: "These were all commended for their faith, yet none of them received what had been promised. God had planned something better for us so that only together with us would they be made perfect" (vv. 39–40).

The rewards of some may even be greater in the future life because they suffered when there was no relief in sight. They believed and trusted, even when they were not delivered.

We need to realize that when God allows these things to happen, there is a reason that will eventually be known to us—perhaps not until we get to Heaven.

Can We Profit from Pain?

Marine Lieutenant Clebe McClary was in a stationary combat observation post deep in enemy-controlled territory in Vietnam. In five months as patrol leader, he hadn't lost a man. He never thought he would be hit. He had no dark premonitions about his mission one night in 1968, but enemy grenades targeted his foxhole. That night he lost his left hand, his left eye, and one leg. As he described it, "Death looked me over—a helpless heap of bleeding flesh and broken bones."

McClary did live, a miracle of God's grace. Although a "religious" man, it was not until he left the hospital on his first leave and went to a stadium in South Carolina, where he heard evangelist Billy Zeoli preach the Gospel, that he invited Jesus Christ into his heart. A year later McClary gave his testimony at our Crusade in Anaheim, California, where he shared with fifty-six thousand people what God had done in his life.

Did Clebe McClary profit from the horrible ordeal that left him disabled for life? This is what he wrote: "I don't think my suffering was in vain. The Lord has used my experiences for good by drawing many lives to Him. It's hard to see any good that came from the war in Vietnam, but I don't believe our effort was wasted. Surely some seed was planted for Christ that cannot be stamped out."[3]

The Apostle Peter tells the reason for trials and persecutions: "These have come so that your faith—of greater worth than gold, which perishes even though refined by fire—may be proved genuine and may result in praise, glory and honor when Jesus Christ is revealed" (1 Peter 1:7).

Remember Job? If ever a man had trials, it was this fellow. But this is what he concluded: "When he has tested me, I will come forth as gold" (Job 23:10). That is reacting positively to testing, building on it, rather than criticizing it for interfering with life's normal pattern.

Trials that often come into a Christian's life are the fulfillment of God's gracious purpose as He seeks to make us the sort of person He planned for us to be when He first thought of us. Like a sculptor, He begins with a lump of marble. But He has in mind a picture of what He intends to create. He breaks, cracks, chisels, and polishes until one day there emerges His vision, like Michelangelo's *David.* At the moment, His sculpture of us is incomplete. God has not yet finished with us.

To Lead Us to the Bible

Martin Luther said, "Were it not for tribulation I should not understand Scripture." Bible study may become a routine, dull experience when placed on a daily "things to do" list. But how fast we learn in a day of sorrow or when problems arise! We become aware of how ignorant we are of Bible promises until we are driven to the Scriptures in times of trial.

Joni Eareckson Tada described what she felt as she lay completely helpless in the hospital. She wrote in her book *Joni* that for the first time she saw meaning in the Bible. "My own 'fiery trials' were now a little easier to cope with as I saw how I fit in with God's scheme of things, especially through reading the Psalms." Joni personalized David's words from Psalm 41:3—"The Lord will sustain [me] on [my] sickbed."

A young woman whose younger brother was killed told how she picked up her Bible and, with eyes blurred with tears, read until she came across a certain verse. She called her heartbroken mother and said, "Mom, listen to this verse. 'If we live, we live to the Lord; and if we die, we die to the Lord. So whether we live or die, we belong to the Lord' (Romans 14:8). Mom, it's OK. I know where Bob is."

When we are first hit by pain, disappointment, sorrow, or grief, we may be overwhelmed. We are stunned and unable to see any good out of our disaster. But before long, with patience in reading the Word of God, we may be able to say with David: "The punishment you gave me was the best thing that could have happened to me, for it taught me to pay attention to your laws. They are more valuable to me than millions in silver and gold" (Psalm 119:71–72 TLB).

To Deepen Our Fellowship with God

Nothing will drive us to our knees quicker than trouble. When war was being waged in the Persian Gulf more was heard about prayer than in any recent year. Even hardened newsmen were talking about prayer.

God hears the prayers of those who recognize Jesus Christ as their personal Savior, but our prayers must be in accordance with His will. He knows better what is good for us than we know ourselves.

Too often we neglect the privilege of prayer until we encounter suffering or difficulty. Some of the greatest prayer warriors I know are dear saints in nursing homes or hospital beds. My mother was a wonderful example of a Christian who knew how to pray. In her last years, not able to take care of herself and in constant pain, she believed the only reason the Lord was delaying His coming for her was so she could pray for others. It was an amazing ministry. Whenever she heard of someone in need she would have Rose, her companion, write a note and send a few dollars.

I was in France for a Crusade, and I called my mother's home. Rose said Mother had given her the Scripture for the day, Colossians 1:9. "For this cause we also, since the day we heard it, do not cease to pray for you, and to desire that ye might be filled with the knowledge of his will in all wisdom and spiritual understanding" (KJV). While I was concerned about my dear mother, thousands of miles away on a bed of weakness and pain, she had a verse of encouragement for me.

Suffering Teaches Us Patience

A woman who lived with pain said that she could not live "one day at a time," as her doctor told her. "I live one moment at a time, knowing that I can stand that much pain. When that moment is gone, I can live for another moment."

> *Too often we neglect the privilege of prayer until we encounter suffering or difficulty.*

Helen Keller said, "Face your deficiencies and acknowledge them, but do not let them master you. Let them teach you patience, sweetness, insight. When we do the best we can, we never know what miracle is wrought in our own life or in the life of another."[4]

In Zephaniah 3:17, we find in the margin notes of the King James Version these words from the Hebrew: "He will be silent in His love." Sometimes God seems so quiet. However, when we see the way He works in lives that are imprisoned by walls or circumstances, when we hear how faith can shine through uncertainty, we begin to catch a glimpse of the fruit of patience that can grow out of the experience of suffering.

Peter says, "How is it to your credit if you receive a beating for doing wrong and endure it? But if you suffer for doing good and you endure it, this is commendable before God" (1 Peter 2:20). People suffer and ask God for an explanation. They often quote (or are quoted) one of my favorite verses, Romans 8:28: "We know that in all things God works for the good of those who love him, who have been called according to his purpose." Christians look at the circumstances and say, "How can this possibly work together for my good?" We can't answer that. Only God can make it work for good, and He can't do it unless we cooperate with Him. In all of our praying we must ask that His will be done.

Calvin Thielman, the pastor of the church where we live, illustrated Romans 8:28 this way. Taken individually, the ingredients in a cake may not taste very good. Raw flour is not good! Baking powder, raw eggs, bitter chocolate, or shortening are not good. Any one of these by itself does not taste good, but they work together to make a delicious cake. In the same way, God puts together the individual trials we have and works them for good.

I am not a person who believes we should cancel our newspapers and cut off our televisions so that we do not know what is happening in the world. But when I see the terrible injustice, the cruelty, the numbing madness that exists, we cannot help but ask, "Has the world gone crazy?"

It is reassuring to know that God is still all-powerful, that nothing touches my life without His permission. Things happen to me that I cannot understand, but I never doubt God's love. In the hour of trial I may not be able to see His design, but I am confident it must be in line with His purpose.

The real philosophical stumper is, "Why, in the midst of madness and rebellion in the world, where sin is glorified and good is degraded, why should God send His only begotten Son to love, heal, comfort, and after thirty-three years of teaching and service, to have Him give His life for this very world?"

When the brilliant Swiss theologian Karl Barth was asked by a group of young theologians what was the most important theological fact he had discovered during his lifetime of studies, the old scholar puffed silently on his pipe as he thoughtfully studied the question. The students sat silent, breathless with expectation. Finally, he removed his pipe, paused, and said simply, "Jesus loves me, this I know, for the Bible tells me so!"

The mystery of God's love would not be a mystery if we knew all the answers. Without faith it is impossible to please God. What we do possess are the answers the Bible gives, and from that basis we have the opportunity to share the love of Christ Himself.

It is critical that we either answer or learn to live with these questions, because like the pain that raises them, they are unavoidable. The Apostle Paul lived with these same questions, but he used them to increase his faith rather than allow them to diminish it. He said that now we see as though we were looking through a cloudy mirror, but one day it will be clear to us.

In the first little book she wrote, long before she became known throughout the world, Corrie ten Boom told of her experience in Ravensbruk prison during World War II:

> I did not understand the "why" of suffering, except that of my own suffering in this place. God had brought me here for a specific task. I was here to lead the sorrowing and the despairing to the Savior. I was to see how He comforted them. I was to point the way to Heaven to people among whom were many that would soon be dying. . . . The "why" of my own suffering was no problem to me.
>
> This, too, I had learned: that I was not called upon to bear the grief and the cares of the whole world around me. And so I prayed, "Lord teach me to cast all my burdens upon Thee and go on without them. Only Thy Spirit can teach me that lesson. Give me Thy Spirit, O Lord, and I shall have faith, such faith that I shall no longer carry a load of care."[5]

Where is God when we suffer? He is ever-present and all-knowing, with us in all our struggles and trials. Nothing in our lives takes God by surprise. We are not alone in our suffering, for we have a God who loves us, "a very present help in trouble."

> "*In all of our praying we must ask that His will be done.*"

God is in control. He may not take away trials or make detours for us, but He strengthens us through them.

8

What Do I Do When I Hurt?

Sometimes the Lord calms the storm; sometimes He lets the storm rage and calms the child.

—unknown

PAIN CAN DRIVE US IN TWO DIRECTIONS. Either it can make us curse God for allowing our misery, or drive us to Him for relief. There is the expression, "God helps those who help themselves." I think a saying like "God helps us when we are helpless" is infinitely more comforting.

Sickness teaches us that activity is not the only way to serve God. "They also serve who only stand and wait." Man seems to judge active duty, but God shows us that He is also glorified through suffering.

Linda had been poisoned by chemicals, resulting in the destruction of her immune system, making her "allergic to the world." She was like the "boy in the bubble" who lived in a plastic enclosure to guard him from every atmospheric contaminant. Linda was in and out of intensive care and isolation units for five years of her young adult life. She said, "Most of the time I didn't think coherently. I was too busy trying to survive."

Linda struggled with one small goal during those years of intense suffering. She read one verse of Scripture each day and prayed for one minute. "And that was an overwhelming task," she said.

When she was able to leave the prison of hospital isolation, she began to reach out to others. She founded an organization called Direct Link, which links a disabled person to a source of help and support. She said, "The Lord gave me suffering so that I could help the suffering world of the disabled."

Jesus said, "What I tell you in the dark, speak in the daylight" (Matthew 10:27). What does this mean to us? It means, be quiet, listen to God when things are their worst, and you will be able to talk to others when you are better.

Oswald Chambers explained, "Watch where God puts you in darkness, and when you are there keep your mouth shut. . . . Darkness is the time to listen and heed. If you talk to other people, you cannot hear what God is saying. When you are in the dark, listen, and God will give you a very precious message for someone else when you get in the light."[1]

Reactions to pain are as varied as pain itself. Many people say that women can bear more pain than men. In fact, one person wrote: "Man endures pain as an undeserved punishment; woman accepts it as a natural heritage." Having watched women in pain, I believe that is true. Most wives can vouch for that.

Resentment Is a Killer

Resentment leads to bitterness. For example, Lord Byron and Sir Walter Scott were gifted writers and poets who lived in the late eighteenth and early nineteenth centuries. They were both lame. Byron bitterly resented his infirmity and constantly grumbled about his lot in life. Scott was never heard to complain about his handicap.

One day Scott received a letter from Byron that said, "I would give my fame to have your happiness." What made the difference in their reactions to suffering and their attitudes toward their disabilities? Byron was a man who took pride in his dissolute lifestyle. His moral standards were doubtful. Scott, on the other hand, was a Christian believer whose courageous life exemplified his standards and values.

A friend of ours, whose husband had left her after fifty years of marriage for a girl young enough to be his granddaughter, asked us once, "What does one do with bitterness?" Bitterness is like an abscess. It festers and grows, and has to come to a head, which is an extremely painful process. But once it is ripe, it will either burst or require lancing, which will get rid of all the poison. Even so, it still takes time for the wound to heal, and there will always be a scar.

Bitterness can strangle a human being. It can turn those who are in pain into complaining, self-pitying people who eventually drive others away. The Bible says, "See to it that no one misses the grace of God and that no bitter root grows up to cause trouble and defile many" (Hebrews 12:15).

Betty was a tiny woman, but her influence upon her daughter and grandchildren was profound. From the time her husband died, she was sick. She diagnosed herself with every ailment in her home medical guide. Her daughter was kept constantly in tension, because Betty would call her with emergencies night and day. Her grandchildren never enjoyed her visits. She resented the fact that her sicknesses, real or imaginary, made her dependent upon her family. And she drove her family away from her.

If we are living self-centered lives and something happens to disrupt our carefully laid plans, our natural tendency is to react with impatience and resentment. We tend to blame God when things go wrong and take credit when things seem to be going right. This may become a way of life with us, as it was with Betty, and the result is unattractive and repelling.

Resentment and bitterness develop when we persist in resisting what God has allowed to happen to us. Christians who are strong in the faith grow as they accept whatever God allows to enter their lives. Resentment can compound physical pain. The steps are short from stress to tension, and pain becomes more severe.

To resent and resist God's disciplining hand is to miss one of the greatest spiritual blessings we Christians can enjoy this side of Heaven. Though Job suffered as few others have, he never lost sight of God's presence with him in the midst of suffering. He emerged victorious on the other side of sorrow, because he never allowed resentment to cloud his relationship with God.

Resentment leaves us with an embittered personality, but there is another response that sounds so noble and pious. This is heard in the sighs of the self-made martyr!

Suffering with a Sigh

With a deep breath, the sufferer approaches daily living with doleful resignation. Let's admit it, most of us feel this way at some point in our lives. "It's just something I have to live with," we say with a forced smile. But resignation is not a distinctly Christian virtue. The Stoics of ancient Greece accepted calamity with resignation as the hallmark of their philosophy. Often resignation is the easy way out, a sort of painkiller—anesthesia where there should be action.

We've probably all experienced times when we feel we should "keep a stiff upper lip," or wear a happy face button on our lapel when we're crying on the inside. I'm glad David didn't live on a perpetual high. Think of the Psalms we would have missed if he had said, "Don't worry about me, folks, everything is just great." David complained, cried, and felt abandoned, but not perpetually.

Christians seem to be programmed to keep suffering to themselves. But God will hear our complaints, and the wonderful thing is that He won't hold them against us.

David refused to resign himself to the defeats that sometimes threatened to flatten him. More than once, in his personal as well as his public life, he seemed to be "down for the count"—but he always looked beyond the obstacle or problem to God Himself. When we're "in the pits," we don't need to resign ourselves to fate or tough luck, but say, "I lift up my eyes to the hills—where does my help come from? My help comes from the Lord, the Maker of heaven and earth" (Psalm 121:1–2).

> "*Christians who are strong in the faith grow as they accept whatever God allows to enter their lives.*"

If we have our eyes upon ourselves, our problems, and our pain, we cannot lift our eyes upward. A child looks up when he's walking with his father, and the same should be true for the Christian.

Unfortunately, in our society there is little tolerance for another's sickness or pain. We put sick people out of sight, or at least out of mind. Resentment builds when we are not treated as someone of value. Many people with long-term illnesses tell how they get cards and calls in the first few days or weeks of their sickness. But too soon the mailbox is empty, the phone silent, and the visitors dwindle. Loneliness is foisted upon someone who is suffering because those who are healthy don't want to be bothered.

Sometimes our burdens seem too big for anyone to handle. We are buried in the quicksand of physical and emotional pain. Jesus reaches out with a love that never fails, never forgets, and is always available and says, "Come to me, all you who are weary and burdened and I will give you rest. Take my yoke upon you and learn from me, for I am gentle and humble in heart, and you will find rest for your souls. For my yoke is easy and my burden is light" (Matthew 11:28–30).

Come. Take. Learn. What powerful words! They contain an invitation to accept and take advantage of our burdens and our hurts. A muscle becomes weak if it is not used. To become strong, a muscle must push against something. To reach the greatest heights as an individual, a person must learn how to take advantage of difficulty.

Dave Dravecky, former star pitcher for the San Francisco Giants, made a remarkable comeback after cancer surgery and was giving speeches around the country about overcoming adversity. After having 50 percent of the major pitching muscle removed from his left arm, he used that arm to throw eight strong innings and defeat the Cincinnati Reds, 4–3. At the time a tearful Dravecky said, "It's a miracle."

Five days after this triumph, his left arm broke. He was out for the season, but he thought he could make another comeback. That dream was shattered when the doctors discovered a mass in his arm that resembled another cancerous tumor.

Dravecky said, "Nobody ever promised that life would be fair. Everybody is going to have adversity. The only way to handle it is to take our eyes off our own circumstances and put them on the Lord."[2]

Comfort and prosperity have never enriched the world as much as adversity has done. Out of pain and problems have come the sweetest songs, the most poignant poems, and the most gripping stories. When we have visited our oldest daughter, who married a Swiss, we have taken chairlifts high up in the Alps to see the scenery. I am not a skier, so our trips are usually in the summer. We gaze down from dizzying heights and see some of the most beautiful flowers found anywhere. It's hard to believe that just a few weeks before, these flowers were buried under many feet of snow. The burdens of ice and winter storms have added to their luster and growth.

> *Comfort and prosperity have never enriched the world as much as adversity has done.*

Our burdens can have the same effect on our lives. As Christians face the winds of adversity and the storms of trouble, they may rise with more beauty. They are like the trees that grow on the mountain ridges of North Carolina—battered by winds, yet trees in which we find the strongest wood.

Resentment and resignation are not the answer to the problem of suffering. Accepting our lot in life and clinging to the Lord and His strength will ease our pain. There is another step beyond acceptance, and that is acceptance with joy. Is it possible?

It's All in the Attitude

When Jeff Steinberg limped onstage, the audience seemed to suck in its breath. His body was tragically misshapen, and it was difficult for him to walk. His head was disproportionately large for his body, and he held a microphone with the hooks he used for hands. But his smile was bigger than his disability. Jeff Steinberg had a song and a slogan that was uniquely his: "I'm a masterpiece in progress."

Instead of focusing on his physical problems, he looked at the gifts God had given him and used them fully. He could laugh, he could sing, and he could tell about God's love.

We don't have a magic shield to protect us from problems. Ultimately, it's our attitude that counts—attitude toward ourselves and toward God. We can turn burdens into blessings, or we can let those burdens bury us.

James said, "Consider it pure joy, my brothers, whenever you face trials of many kinds, because you know that the testing of your faith develops perseverance. Perseverance must finish its work so that you may be mature and complete, not lacking anything" (James 1:2–4).

Joy is one of the marks of a true believer. This is not a gushy emotion or a forced grin, but the security of knowing God's love. I read a news story about soldiers in the Persian Gulf watching videotapes from their families back home. In a gloomy tent, sipping coffee to ward off the morning chill, the soldiers listened in silence as one wife held herself erect and sang a gospel hymn that her husband could think of whenever he felt alone. Joy is not just jumping up and down when your team makes a touchdown, it's that deep, abiding emotion that gives a lonely soldier's wife the ability to reach out to an equally lonely man and touch him with God's presence. The ability to rejoice in any situation is a sign of spiritual maturity.

Paul sang and shouted his way through his trials. His greatest victories came out of his persecution. To the Romans he wrote, "We also rejoice in our sufferings, because we know that suffering produces perseverance. . . . Who shall separate us from the love of Christ? Shall trouble or hardship or persecution? . . . Be joyful in hope, patient in affliction, faithful in prayer" (Romans 5:3; 8:35; 12:12).

Grady Wilson was one of my closest friends, as well as associate and traveling companion. He was always able to see the funny side of things and make me laugh. He was a person who radiated joy, and anyone he ever met would quickly find out that "count it all joy" was his favorite expression.

We all know people who are not Christians who seem to possess the key to joy, but that soon evaporates when the tough times come. On the other hand, we know professing Christians who look as if they habitually eat lemons. These are the people who fight God's will for their lives and complain that life has dealt them unfair blows. Christ Himself is the Christian's secret of joy: "Though you have not seen him, you love him, and even though you do not see him now, you believe in him and are filled with an inexpressible and glorious joy" (1 Peter 1:8).

"

The ability to rejoice in any situation is a sign of spiritual maturity.

"

I remember visiting an elderly man who spent most of his life in China as a missionary. He had always enjoyed good health and was an unusually strong man. His deep dedication to Christ and the love between him and his wife made people love and admire him. However, he contracted cancer, and it spread to many parts of his body. I went to minister to him, but, instead, he ministered to me. There was a joy and radiance about him that I have rarely seen. He got up out of his bed and walked me to the car when I left. I shall never forget my last glimpse of him. With a great smile and cheery wave, he said, "Keep on preaching the Gospel, Billy. The older I get, the better Christ is to me."

When we are so wedded to the world that we lose sight of eternity, we can lose our joy. My father-in-law, Nelson Bell, held on to the things of this world so loosely that when he died and we opened his closet, there were only two suits hanging there. Things were not that important to him.

In my travels I have found that those who keep Heaven in view remain serene and cheerful in the darkest day. If the glories of Heaven were more real to us, if we lived less for material things and more for things eternal and spiritual, we would be less easily disturbed by this present life.

A friend told me about stopping on a street corner in London and listening to a man play the bagpipes. He was playing "Amazing Grace" and smiling from ear to ear. My friend asked him if he was from Scotland, and he answered, "No sir, my home is in Heaven. I'm just traveling through this world."

Closer My God to Thee or Farther Away?

How do we respond to crisis or suffering? We can resent suffering, resign ourselves to it, or accept it with joy because we know God is in control of our lives.

Amy Carmichael, who lived in almost constant pain, is a striking example of a Christian whose physical suffering enabled her to reflect the character of Christ. She lived her life rejoicing in the midst of tribulation. She wrote this poem:

Before the winds that blow do cease,
  Teach me to dwell within Thy calm:
Before the pain has passed in peace,
  Give me, my God, to sing a psalm.
Let me not lose the chance to prove
  The fullness of enabling love.
O Love of God, do this for me:
  Maintain a constant victory.[3]

Rewards Here and Later

We're living in a time of spiritual darkness and political upheaval. Only the forward-looking Christian remains sincerely optimistic and joyful, knowing that Christ will win in the end and "if we endure, we will also reign with him" (2 Timothy 2:12).

God works in unexpected ways to bring us strength and joy in the midst of suffering. The Scriptures say, "Now is your time of grief, but I will see you again and you will rejoice, and no one will take away your joy" (John 16:22), and "For our light and momentary troubles are achieving for us an eternal glory that far outweighs them all" (2 Corinthians 4:17).

There is a joy to be discovered in the midst of suffering. I truly believe that the lot of those that suffer is more enviable than the people who seem to be set apart, untouched, like a piece of fine china in a locked cabinet. Without dark clouds in our lives we would never know the joy of sunshine. We can become callous and unteachable if we do not learn from pain.

It is said that if your cup seems too bitter, if your burden seems too heavy, be sure that it is the wounded hand that is holding the cup and that it is He who carried the cross that is carrying the burden with us. "Come unto me, all ye that labour and are heavy laden," He says, "and I will give you rest. Take my yoke upon you, and learn of me. . . . For my yoke is easy, and my burden is light" (Matthew 11:28–30 KJV).

9

When Your Heart Is Breaking

I will search for the lost and bring back the strays. I will bind up the injured and strengthen the weak.

Ezekiel 34:16

IT WAS THE MESSAGE SHE MOST FEARED. The young wife of a corporal serving in the Persian Gulf was told that her husband had been instantly killed in Saudi Arabia by a missile. She said, "I'll never forget the nauseating feeling when I opened my door and heard that news."

Your heart may be breaking with grief over the death of a loved one. You may have a child with a long-term illness or one who has left home in open rebellion. Perhaps you have lost your job or experienced a crushing failure in your personal life. Maybe you just want to help relieve someone else's pain.

In *Hope for the Hurting,* Doug Sparks wrote about the griefs we encounter: "If you don't have one now, you will. If you live long enough, there'll come a time when you have to keep going even though your heart is pierced through."[1] Somehow we have to keep on keeping on.

My wife grew up in China, but I have never been able to master the language. The Chinese system of writing contains pictographs, characters that represent mental images, and I have been told that the Chinese word picture for perseverance is represented by a knife and a heart. How true that is in our personal experiences. What do you do when you feel ripped in half? How do you continue (persevere) with a knife in your heart?

Many Faces of Grief

Barbara Johnson's Marine son was killed in Vietnam. Five years later, her oldest boy was hit and killed by a drunk driver. Two years later, on the eve of another son's graduation from a junior college, where he had been voted the most outstanding student, he told his mother he was a homosexual. Grief compounded upon grief. The knife in her heart was so sharp she thought she would die. She wrote: "I think I'm having a heart attack. I don't know what you call it, but I think I'm dying. I can't breathe, and I'm choking. It feels as if I've got a rug in my throat and my teeth itch."[2]

When Barbara Johnson described her reactions as a Christian, she said, "All the promises of God are there, and they're real, and they're true, but right now you're bleeding, you're raw and hurting, and you have to hang on to those promises even if they don't seem to work for you at the moment."[3]

Responses to grief are as varied as grief itself. While some people want to die, others blow up. They shout and curse the world and blaspheme God. Sociologists have tried to grade the types of grief according to their severity, but no one can put a magnifying glass on another's hurts, except God.

Many times grief is accompanied by guilt; whether real or false, guilt compounds grief. With false guilt, we fall into the trap of "if only's." "If only we had been home, we might have been able to get the paramedics in time." "If only we hadn't said she could stay out until midnight." These thoughts are normal emotions when we feel guilty about something over which we have no control.

Then there is real guilt. Emotions become raw when we know we have disobeyed man's or God's laws or have become careless with what God has given us.

One vivid example of guilt due to carelessness was the news story about the man who was driving his family to the market, a few blocks from his home. His wife was holding their baby instead of having him confined to a car seat. The father made a left turn and accidentally ran into an oncoming car, resulting in a crushing impact. The baby was thrown against the windshield, killing him instantly. Soon after the accident, the distraught father was charged with manslaughter, because he hadn't obeyed the law requiring safety seats for children under the age of four. Imagine the amount of grief compounded by guilt in that poor father's heart.

How can we understand the grief of others unless we have been in their shoes? Jesus was no stranger to grief. It was foretold by Isaiah that He would be a "man of sorrows and acquainted with grief." Our greatest hope is that people may know Him before an hour of severe grief.

> "*Many times grief is accompanied by guilt; whether real or false, guilt compounds grief.*"

Some people may have an outward appearance of serenity and peace after a tragedy or severe loss, but inside they may be hemorrhaging. Grief may drive them to resentment or blaming others. We can almost imagine the tone of Martha's voice when, after her brother Lazarus died, she said to Jesus, "Lord, if you had been here my brother would not have died" (John 11:32). She was indulging in the "if only's" that plague many of us.

Jesus didn't try to reason with Martha or argue with her. He understood her frustration. If there is something we need more than anything else during grief, it is a friend who stands with us, who doesn't leave us. Jesus is that friend.

The faces of grief may be filled with anger. Anger is debilitating if it runs unchecked. Non-Christians may vent their anger like animals with snarling, destructive, cruel acts. Before we put on faces of piety, we must realize that Christians are not above some of these attitudes. They often can be just as vehement as their non-Christian neighbors.

King David cried out, "Why are you downcast, O my soul? Why so disturbed within me?" (Psalm 42:5). David was distraught. His very soul was in turmoil. Have you ever felt that way? Have you ever been so down in the dumps that you couldn't see a way to climb out? Grief can kill a person emotionally and physically. If not counteracted with God's strength and power, our personal weakness may debilitate us.

Another face of grief is panic. "I imagine all sorts of terrible things. I think I'm losing my mind." The grief-stricken person seems to lose the ability to concentrate, which adds to his panic. Panic may lead to emotional paralysis.

Guilt, anger, resentment, panic. These are just some of the faces of grief. None of these reactions are abnormal. Like soldiers going into battle, we need to be prepared for grief.

A clipping from the war in the Persian Gulf explained how a veteran officer prepared his troops for the possibility of a bloody ground war. Until that time none of these soldiers, except the battalion commander, had ever seen real combat. He told them, "I want to talk about fear. You will be afraid. If you're not afraid, there's something wrong with you . . . you'll know when you're afraid, guys . . . you will taste a metal taste in your mouth like you had maybe a half-dozen nails. It is going to happen. Understand it. Cope with it. Talk to each other about it. Understand with each other that all of you are afraid . . . all you can do is have faith in the guys around you. I have faith in you. I know you'll do the best you can. Have faith in me to do my best."[4]

"

If there is something we need more than anything else during grief, it is a friend who stands with us, who doesn't leave us. Jesus is that friend.

"

That officer was preparing his men for combat, just as our Lord prepares us for life's combat. I don't know how anyone overcomes personal grief without His directions. He says to have faith in Him. He has told us that He will be with us always and never leave or forsake us (Hebrews 13:5).

Often it takes that "knife in our heart" to drive us to Him. Our faith, our very lives, depend on God, and when we enter the valley of grief, we need His help or we will never climb another mountain.

Wounded Hearts

Remember how we used to chant, "Sticks and stones will break my bones, but words will never hurt me?" That's not true. Probably some of the worst pain is caused by wounds from others, words or actions that break our lives into fractured pieces.

Henry had worked for the same company for more than thirty years. He had been a valuable member of the firm, loyal to the core, and dependable. He was close to retirement, and his pension was going to be the major part of his living expenses. Henry was given his severance notice due to a change in company management. He went home, a broken man, too shocked to know what to do next.

We have been given the ability to hope and dream, to set goals and make plans for what we want our lives to be. What do we do when someone else takes our dreams and smashes them into pieces?

Our children may wound us and twist the knife in our heart until we believe we will never be able to heal. David Jeremiah wrote about the painful time he experienced when his daughter was caught experimenting with cocaine at the Christian school where he was president. He wrote, "The feelings that overwhelmed me . . . were unlike anything in my previous experience . . . nothing in my life had prepared me for the initial shock and the resulting pain of the days and months to follow."[5]

When we think we've done our best as parents and things go wrong, the wounds we receive may turn to guilt. "Where did we go wrong?" we cry. I have met godly men and women who have suffered heartache as a result of wounds from their children. The healing of these wounds can only come when we love our children unconditionally, release the guilt feelings, and get on with the recovery.

People cause wounds, and usually we don't blame God when we have people problems. A friend divulges a confidence or spreads an untruth about us. A promise is broken or words are spoken to us in anger. Let's face it, so many of our problems are caused by people who take advantage of us, misuse us, or are just plain hard to get along with.

Does Jesus understand these wounds? He was misunderstood, scorned, ignored, and finally betrayed. Remember the old spiritual, "Nobody knows the troubles I've seen . . . nobody knows but Jesus"? He said, "Whatever you did for one of the least of these brothers of mine, you did for me" (Matthew 25:40). I believe that applies to the problem people in our lives, as well as the hungry, the thirsty, the stranger, the naked and sick, and the imprisoned. "One of the least of these brothers" may be the very person who has been a thorn in your side and who needs your unconditional love.

Many Faces of Persecution

Persecution may wear an insulting face. Insults may come as a result of a Christian's lifestyle, which should be different from that of the secular world. Peter said: "If you are insulted because of the name of Christ, you are blessed, for the Spirit of glory and of God rests on you" (1 Peter 4:14).

> *"Let's face it, so many of our problems are caused by people who take advantage of us, misuse us, or are just plain hard to get along with."*

If the Bible says, "Thou shalt not . . . ," then there's no doubt. However, if the Bible is not explicit, then we should weigh the pros and cons and ask God to give us wisdom to do what would please Him under the circumstances.

Christians are being persecuted today for holding their basic beliefs, and even in the United States they are persecuted for their stands on moral issues. If your heart is wounded by insults, know that Jesus blesses you. He said, "Blessed are you when people insult you, persecute you and falsely say all kinds of evil against you because of me" (Matthew 5:11).

It's a small step "from insult to injury," and one of the worst wounds we can receive or give is done with words. Snide words, critical words, unkind words, untrue words. The twin ills caused by the tongue can infect Christian and non-Christian alike. If a Christian makes a mistake in his life, he is more vulnerable than a non-Christian. Churches have been split by gossip. Families have been broken by slander. Ministries have been destroyed by the indiscretions of a few.

Christians may be slandered because they hold to their beliefs. A Christian student at a high school or college is verbally abused because he wouldn't join his peers in a drinking or sex party. The Christian businessman loses an account because he wouldn't take a kickback. The Christian salesman was honest in his expense accounts and was laughed at by his fellow salesmen. It costs in a thousand subtle ways to be a true disciple of Christ. Peter expressed it so well: "They think it strange that you do not plunge with them into the same flood of dissipation, and they heap abuse on you" (1 Peter 4:4).

If we are living according to what we believe, we may be falsely accused. It is not to our credit, however, if we are accused because our conduct as believers is inconsistent. Jesus was falsely accused at His trial. The Apostles Peter and John were falsely accused when they were brought before the Council. Stephen was falsely accused and lost his life. If the apostles and other early church leaders were falsely accused because of their faith, how can we expect to escape false accusations and the hurt that such attacks can bring into our lives?

Have you ever been rejected? Probably one of the forms of persecution that hurts the most is rejection. Basically, we all want to be accepted and loved. But there are very few people I have known who haven't had some rejection in their lives. The hardest to take is when it comes from a member of your family, a close friend, or perhaps worst of all, from your husband or wife.

During the Persian Gulf War many young men and women accepted Christ. The chaplains have told of unprecedented numbers of soldiers attending services, making commitments, and being baptized. When these new Christians return to their homes, they may be accused of "foxhole religion" by the ones they love.

I was on an airliner in the Far East when one of the stewards asked if he could talk to me. He had a big smile on his face when he said, "I have been a Christian for two years. I came from a non-Christian background. My family belonged to a religious sect that was quite opposed to Christianity. Yet for years I had been searching for something. I didn't know what it was. One day I listened to a tape of a preacher who told about Jesus Christ. I knew this was what I had been searching for all my life. I accepted Christ, went home and told my parents, brothers, and sisters about my newfound faith. They threw me out of the house. However, I continued to witness to them and now, I am glad to say, they are all Christians."

Recently I met a man with a strong, but tragic face. It was just a year ago, I was told, that his son had been shot to death in front of his home by religious extremists. The man's eyes filled, and as the tears coursed down his cheeks, I suggested we pray. I, who have suffered so little and nothing like he has, felt unworthy to pray. Later, I learned he could not return home as these same extremists had threatened to kill him. Out of fear, his wife has rejected both him and the Christian faith. He had no job, no money, no home. That is what persecution is like.

Jesus told His disciples that the "world," meaning the world system, the political and social order organized apart from God, will despise Christians. He said, "If the world hates you, keep in mind that it hated me first. If you belonged to the world, it would love you as its own" (John 15:18–19).

Can You Relate to Paul?

When we're hurting from what could be called the subtle suffering of life, we may find little comfort that others are experiencing or have experienced the same trials. The Apostle Paul was in the major leagues when it comes to all types of suffering. What a list he had:

> For it seems to me that God has put us apostles on display at the end of the procession, like men condemned to die in the arena. We have been made a spectacle to the whole universe, to angels as well as to men. We are fools for Christ, but you are so wise in Christ! We are weak, but you are strong! You are honored, we are dishonored! To this very hour we go hungry and thirsty, we are in rags, we are brutally treated, we are homeless. We work hard with our own hands. When we are cursed, we bless; when we are persecuted, we endure it; when we are slandered, we answer kindly. Up to this moment we have become the scum of the earth, the refuse of the world.
>
> *1 Corinthians 4:9–13*

Paul had devastating physical sufferings, but he described even greater pressure as he thought about his responsibilities as a Christian missionary. "I face daily the pressure of my concern for all the churches" (2 Corinthians 11:28).

If any of you are leaders in your churches or Christian organizations, you know the kind of pressure Paul is describing. Humanly speaking, it can lead to loneliness, depression, and often discouragement. Only God's illimitable grace and peace can carry us through times of trial.

In my own life, the pressures at times, mentally, physically, and spiritually, have become so great that I felt like going to the Cove and lying down in the cemetery to see how I fit. God has called me to my responsibilities, and I must be faithful. I am constantly concerned about being quoted in the press and perhaps saying the wrong thing or having what I say misinterpreted and bringing reproach to the name of Christ. People put well-known Christians on a pedestal, and if the slightest thing goes wrong, they are immediately blamed and often ridiculed.

> *Only God's illimitable grace and peace can carry us through times of trial.*

At times we do make mistakes. Unintentionally, we offend others. Remember, "we're not offering people Christians, we're offering them Christ." I have wondered what would have happened in the ministry of the Lord Jesus Christ if television had been in existence. What would the media have done, for example, when He drove the moneychangers from the Temple, or when He denounced the Sadducees and Pharisees, or when He raised Lazarus from the dead, or when He fed the five thousand?

Paul's attitude was not that of self-pity, but one of triumph. We can have the same attitude. He said: "We are hard pressed on every side, but not crushed; perplexed, but not in despair; persecuted, but not abandoned; struck down, but not destroyed" (2 Corinthians 4:8–9). God has never sent any difficulty into the life of His children without His accompanying offers of help in this life and reward in the life to come.

David Jacobsen was a hostage in Beirut for seventeen months. He was head of the largest hospital in West Beirut when, one day in 1985, three men in hoods and wielding machine guns took him captive. Bound and gagged, he was taken from one hideout to another. He spent most of his time on a cold, dirt floor, chained to the wall. Once a day he was fed a tepid, unpalatable mush of watery rice and lentils.

As an American, Jacobsen was hated by his captors. He was just a political pawn and treated cruelly. Instead of breaking his spirit, however, he became stronger. He wrote: "I discovered that no one's faith was weakened by the hell we found ourselves in. . . . We hostages, with the guidance of Father Jenko, a captive Catholic priest, and Rev. Benjamin Weir, founded the Church of the Locked Door, a name we chose with some ruefulness. Grasping hands, we'd quote Scripture and pray. Oddly, our guards seemed to respect this ritual. Our togetherness in prayer showed me that when the Holy Comforter is called, He answers."

Jacobsen was released in November 1986, but in his final forty-five days of captivity he was alone in a six-by-six-by-six cell, his muscles and joints cramped by confinement and the damp, aching cold. Yet he said, "The presence of God, the Great Comforter, was stronger than ever, especially when I recited Psalms 27 and 102."[6]

The Pain of Personal Failure

After reading about other people's triumphs and hearing success stories, we may become more depressed than ever. Even hearing about successful marriages may be bitter if yours is rocky or disintegrating. Success stories may be great motivational material for sales seminars, but we are not always successful. Many people have learned to hide their failures and defeats, not wanting to "bother anyone with my troubles."

Mrs. Charles E. Cowman, in *Streams in the Desert,* says, "Many of us would nurse our grief without crying if we were allowed to nurse it. The hard thing is that most of us are called to exercise our patience, not in bed, but in the street. We are called to bury our sorrows not in lethargic quiescence, but in active service—in the exchange, in the workshop, in the hour of social intercourse, in the contribution to another's joy. There is no burial of sorrow so difficult as that; it is the 'running with patience.'"[7]

Jay Kesler told about a man whose son had been arrested for armed robbery. The story appeared in newspapers and on television. The Christian parents of the boy were so ashamed that they didn't leave their home for several days. Over and over again they asked God how this could happen in their family. They didn't know if they could face people again, particularly those in their church.

The parents finally went to church, and their shame and fear made them stick together like burrs. But something wonderful happened. A constant stream of people started coming to them for spiritual help. The father told Kesler, "It seems to me that when people take a superspiritual pose in church, pretending they have no problems, all the other church people are afraid to be honest with them for fear that they will look like failures. It's really strange that when we were trying our best and, on the surface at least, succeeding in our Christian lives, we didn't touch any other lives. Now that we have had so many problems with our own child, everyone wants our help—everyone wants to know how the Lord is working out our problems."[8]

We hear so many times, "He is a strong Christian." Inside, that person may be very weak, plagued by insecurities, wounded by others. Not knowing, we should encourage each one we meet. The Lord told Paul: "My grace is sufficient for you, for my power is made perfect in weakness. . . . That is why," Paul wrote, "for Christ's sake, I delight in weaknesses, in insults, in hardships, in persecutions, in difficulties. For when I am weak, then I am strong" (2 Corinthians 12:9–10).

We can persevere with a "knife in our heart" when we allow the Lord to lead us, even carrying us in His arms when we are wounded, to the time and place where we will be healed.

The young widow of the soldier mentioned at the beginning of this chapter said that time had helped her look at her situation from a stronger perspective. "You can look at this like the worst thing that ever happened or you can look for something good in this," she said. Someone has said, "You go through it, but you don't get over it." Yet time softens memories, and the presence of Christ helps us not only to survive but to help others. Yes, time does help the broken heart.

Helping others is a great step toward healing. Barbara Johnson now has a ministry that grew out of her own heartbreak. In helping others, she also saw her son denounce his homosexual lifestyle and rededicate his life to Christ. David Jeremiah's daughter was loved through her problems and became a great witness to the healing powers of God.

"Time softens memories, and the presence of Christ helps us not only to survive but to help others."

When we are weak and powerless, God is there to give us strength. When we lack wisdom, He will supply it. Healing is not instantaneous; it is a process. When we admit that we cannot heal ourselves, and we fall to our knees and ask God to take over, we will be on the road to spiritual health. Why wait?

Ruth, who loves the poetry of Amy Carmichael, gave me this one:

Will not the end explain
The crossed endeavor, earnest purpose foiled,
The strange bewilderment of good work spoiled,
The clinging weariness, the inward strain,
Will not the end explain?

Meanwhile He comforteth
Them that are losing patience. 'Tis His way:
But none can write the words they hear Him say
For men to read; only they know He saith
Sweet words, and comforteth.

Not that He doth explain
The mystery that baffleth; but a sense
Husheth the quiet heart, that far, far hence
Lieth a field set thick with golden grain
Wetted in seedling days by many a rain;
The end—it will explain.

10

The Fourth Man in the Fire

When you pass through the rivers,
they will not sweep over you.
When you walk through the fire,
you will not be burned;
the flames will not set you ablaze.
Isaiah 43:2

IN A LAND THAT IS NOW CALLED IRAQ, there was an arrogant, despotic ruler who wanted to be worshiped as a god. He had a golden image of himself erected outside of the capital city of Babylon. He called in his guard and ordered his military band to play for the great ceremony where everyone was ordered to worship his statue. This command was accompanied by a sinister warning. King Nebuchadnezzar gave orders that anyone who didn't bow down would be thrown into a red-hot furnace.

Three Jewish refugees from Jerusalem refused to obey the order. They worshiped their God, not man. They said, "If we are thrown into the blazing furnace, the God we serve is able to save us from it . . . but even if he does not, we want you to know, O king, that we will not serve your gods or worship the image of gold you have set up" (Daniel 3:17–18).

The king was enraged. His order was carried out by his elite guards, and the three Hebrews were thrown into the blazing furnace. But a strange thing happened. The guards were burned to death, and the Jews didn't even have their hair singed. The crowd gasped, the king was shocked, for in the midst of that blazing furnace were seen not three, but four men, walking around unharmed. God was the fourth man in the fire.

God has promised that if we call upon Him, He will be with us in times of trouble. He will walk through our trials with us. He promises to be the other Person with us in the tough times of life, which does not always mean deliverance.

Think of those Christian martyrs who have been burned at the stake, someone who has lost a loved one in a house fire, or an airplane that exploded and crashed in flames. Our Lord could have claimed that promise, "He will give His angels charge over thee." But He was willing, for our sakes, to forego the promise, saying instead, "Thy will be done." For the sake of others, we too at times must be willing to relinquish the promise for His glory and the good of others.

A Book of Promises

The Bible is a book of promises, and unlike the books of men, it doesn't change or get out of date. The message I have been proclaiming for many years is basically the same—and God does not lie!

The Bible makes it clear that no problems in our lives are too great or too small for His concern. He cares about everything that affects His children.

If we have no knowledge of God's promises to us, we will not be able to appropriate them. The three Hebrews, Shadrach, Meshach, and Abednego, had studied their Old Testament Scriptures. Of course, we don't know what promises they claimed when they defied Nebuchadnezzar's order, but it could have been from the Psalms. They might have remembered, "The Lord is my light and my salvation—whom shall I fear?" (27:1). Their words to the king were, "Our God is able to deliver us—*but* if not, we still won't worship your image." They certainly knew some of the promises of God to give them the strength and faith they exhibited.

We cannot possibly cover all the promises of the Bible in this chapter. It would take a book, since figures on the number of biblical promises range from eight thousand to thirty thousand. We just need to know, claim, and memorize a few for the times when we will need them. When it comes to the subject of pain and suffering, there are some promises that God has given us both in the Old and the New Testaments.

When I think of some of the promises, certain people come into my mind. You may have some special promises that the Lord has given you. Hold onto them, cling to them, for you never know when you will need them.

God Promises Us a Refuge

"God is our refuge and our strength, an ever-present help in trouble" (Psalm 46:1). What a great and simple promise! This does not imply that we huddle and are panic-stricken behind a protective wall. It pictures a person actively involved in life, for the psalmist says that God is "ever-present." He goes with His people into the scene of suffering and onto the platform of pain to sustain them in the midst of it.

Refuge means a hiding place, and that always reminds me of a longtime friend whom we met in Switzerland. At one time she was imprisoned by the Nazis and placed in solitary confinement for four months. The cell was dark, with dirty water standing on the floor. When she heard the piercing cries of other prisoners, she knew that she was also under the constant threat of being tortured.

She said: "Once I stood with my back against the wall with my hands spread out, as if to try to push away the walls that were closing in on me. I was dead scared. I cried out, 'Lord, I'm not strong enough to endure this. I don't have the faith.'"

Some of us look at people who have suffered and say, "I wish I had your faith." Corrie admitted to a weak faith, but God spoke to her in an unusual way. She noticed an ant on the floor. The moment that ant felt the water, he ran straight to his tiny hole in the wall.

"Then it was as if the Lord said to me, 'What about that ant? He didn't stop to look at the wet floor or his weak feet—he went straight to his hiding place. Corrie don't look at your faith. It is weak. . . . I am your hiding place, and you can come running to Me just like that ant disappeared into that hole in the wall.'"

From the depths of her despair, Corrie pulled up a verse. She continued her story by speaking to all of us: "I know there are moments for you when you lose all courage. You feel as a prisoner that you don't exist in the eyes of the people around you, in the eyes of God, or in your own eyes. Then you can read in the Bible a promise from Jesus: 'Come to me, all you who are weary and burdened, and I will give you rest' (Matthew 11:28)."[1]

God is our rest, our refuge, our hiding place. In Psalm 91:15 God promises, "He will call upon me, and I will answer him; I will be with him in trouble." Again Scripture says, "Trust in him at all times, O people; pour out your hearts to him, for God is our refuge" (Psalm 62:8).

Sometimes we allow bitterness to replace trust and we can't seem to find God through our pain. We can't seem to pour out our hearts, because they have become so hardened.

A young Irish immigrant, Joseph Scriven (1820–86) was deeply in love with a girl, and their marriage plans had been made. Not long before their wedding day, however, she drowned. For months Scriven was bitter, in utter despair. At last he turned to Christ, and through His grace, he found peace and comfort. Out of this tragic experience he wrote the familiar hymn that has brought consolation to millions of aching hearts: "What a Friend we have in Jesus, all our sins and griefs to bear!"

Sometimes our lives are very bright, as it was for Scriven as he approached his wedding day. But like him, we may find that our path also leads through some dark shadows. Business losses, pensions that don't pay the bills, loss of work, inflation, sickness that lays us low, sorrows that rob our homes of their light, children who rebel—all may be turned into blessings for those who find a hiding place in His love.

He Is Our Shield and Our Refuge

When Moses was about to die, he gave his blessings to the tribes of Israel. To Benjamin he said, "Let the beloved of the Lord rest secure in him, for he shields him all day long, and the one the Lord loves rests between his shoulders" (Deuteronomy 33:12). When children play war they sometimes take the lids off garbage cans and use them for shields. Whatever is thrown at them will bounce off, as long as they use this protection. There will be times in your life when you know the Lord has given you Divine protection.

God is our refuge. He shelters us, just as the eagle spreads its magnificent wings over the nest where the baby birds have been hatched. The eagle is not only protective, but he is strong and courageous. It is no coincidence that the official seal of the United States carries a spread-winged bald eagle.

What an illustration this is for the way God cares for His children! Psalm 91:4 says: "He will cover you with his feathers, and under his wings you will find refuge; his faithfulness will be your shield and rampart."

God Is Our Strength

Dale and Roy Rogers have been friends of mine for many years. They have had many tragedies in their lives, with the deaths of three of their children and setbacks that would stagger most people. In her book, *Trials, Tears, and Triumphs,*

Dale tells a story about having two speaking engagements for large groups on the same day. By the time she had spoken once, she was so emotionally and physically drained that she was sure she would not be able to go on the second time. (I can relate to this!)

Before her second appearance, Dale was overcome with a spell of weakness. She didn't feel she could continue, so she prayed, "Lord, take over, I've had it." That may not be a very profound prayer, but I'm sure many of you have felt the same way. I know I have.

She said, "As I walked into the pastor's study, three young men took my hands and said, 'Let's pray.' We prayed, and strength flowed into me like a mighty river. It sustained me through the entire service. How true it is what Isaiah says: 'They that wait upon the Lord shall renew their strength; they shall mount up with wings as eagles; they shall run, and not be weary; and they shall walk, and not faint' (Isaiah 40:31)."[2] I have heard Dale say that she intends to wear out in His service and not rust out.

Strength. How we need it. Moses told the children of Israel in Deuteronomy 33:25, "Your strength will equal your days." This is a promise for strength in all areas of life. He is our source to go on, not only in the tough times, but for the daily grind. He adds meaning and joy to our days and gives us the strength to go on, or sit still peacefully. Without Him our daily routine would become tiresome and tedious, a drudgery rather than a joy.

He is my strength to go up. The psalmist says, "By my God have I leaped over a wall" (Psalm 18:29 KJV). I cannot literally leap over a wall, unless it's about as high as a curb, but when there are obstacles that look like mountains, He will give us the strength for the climb.

A few good friends who will support us, without a critical attitude, will give us strength when we are down. Having a support group is a valuable asset to carry us when we are buried under a load of troubles. But what if we don't have friends like this? What if we have moved, or there does not seem to be anybody with whom we can be frank and open. What then? Remember, the Holy Spirit is praying (Romans 8:26–27, 34).

Lucinda was going through a very difficult time. She had been sexually abused as a child, and many years later the memory of that terrible time surfaced. She went to a counselor, who helped her with her severe depression and nightmares. But Lucinda moved to another country when her husband's job changed. She was thousands of miles from her counselor and found it difficult to function without the counselor's help and her support group.

“

Having a support group is a valuable asset to carry us when we are buried under a load of troubles.

”

She called one of her Christian friends and said, "I need a simple verse to help me. Can you give me one that's not hard to remember?" Her friend said a quick prayer and went to the Psalms. "Here's one . . . it's Psalm 56:4. 'In God I trust; I will not be afraid. What can mortal man do to me?' " Later, when Lucinda returned to the States, she went back to her counselor. Every time the memories of her abuse surfaced, she repeated that verse.

No matter where we are, God is as close as a prayer. He is our support and our strength. He will help us make our way up again from whatever depths we have fallen.

We don't often consider that sometimes Jesus is our strength simply to sit still. "Be still, and know that I am God" (Psalm 46:10). Our natural tendency when we have a painful happening in our lives is to go into action—do something. Sometimes it is wiser to wait and just be still. The answers will come.

When her husband died, one woman immediately started on a buying spree until most of the life insurance money was gone. Someone else, upon receiving bad news, may react by making other rash and senseless decisions. The Lord is our strength when we allow Him to calm us. "I wait for the Lord, my soul waits, and in his word I put my hope" (Psalm 130:5). "He that hasteth with his foot misses his way" (Proverbs 19:2 ASV).

He Promises to Shepherd Us

The picture of God as a shepherd is found in many places in the Old Testament. What a comfort it is to know that the God of the universe comes down into the hills and valleys of our lives to be our Shepherd.

In the most famous Psalm, David, a former shepherd himself, cries out, "The Lord is *my* shepherd, I shall not be in want" (Psalm 23:1, emphasis added). Our Shepherd leads us, He guides us along the right paths, and He is with us in the dark valley. No wonder David testifies, "My cup overflows" (v. 5). Isaiah describes how the Lord "tends his flock like a shepherd: He gathers the lambs in his arms and carries them close to his heart" (40:11).

In the New Testament Jesus applies the image of the shepherd to Himself. He says, "I am the good shepherd. The good shepherd lays down his life for the sheep. The hired hand is not the shepherd who owns the sheep. So when he sees the wolf coming, he abandons the sheep and runs away. Then the wolf attacks the flock and scatters it. . . . I am the good shepherd; I know my sheep and my sheep know me" (John 10:11–14).

If Jesus lives in the heart, the Good Shepherd owns the sheep; they belong to Him. He guards the sheep; He never leaves them in time of trouble. He knows the sheep by name, and His love is so great that He lays down His life for His sheep.

We need to keep close to our Shepherd, to listen to His voice and follow Him, especially in times of spiritual peril. Jesus tells us not to be misled by the voices of strangers. There are so many strange voices being heard in the religious world of our day. We must compare what they say with the Word of God.

When Jesus Was Jenny's Shepherd

Shame and embarrassment have kept many people from revealing their suffering as the result of sexual abuse and incest. In recent years more and more of these tragic stories have surfaced. All treatment does not fall into the category of psychological counseling, such as Lucinda underwent.

Jenny's mother was a drug dealer. Her parents were divorced, and there was no religious influence in her home. However, when Jenny was three years old, a woman in the apartment building took her to a Good News Club. Jenny began to understand that she had a best friend, and His name was Jesus.

Jenny's mother moved to a large house in an expensive part of the city. Jenny said, "There were as many as thirty people living there at one time. The activities in that house were wicked beyond description, but somehow I felt detached from them, as if there were a shield around me that would not allow me to be touched with this evil."

When her mother was arrested, Jenny was taken to juvenile hall and after that went to live with her father and stepmother in abject poverty. "However, I sought out any church I could find on Sundays and went alone to the services. I loved my Friend so much, and the time spent with Him were my happiest hours."

At the age of twelve, Jenny was sexually abused by a music teacher. She was forced to go to these music lessons, and one time hid in a dumpster to avoid going into the studio. Years later, after pouring herself into her work and putting herself through college, one day the memory of that music teacher flooded over her. "For ten years it had been buried in my subconscious, and when it resurfaced it almost killed me."

Jenny struggled with hatred and guilt, thinking that somehow she was responsible for the molestation, not the victim. She retreated into her house, pulled the blinds, and spent months in solitude. Unlike Lucinda, she did not have the money to pay for a counselor. Instead of seeking outside help, she went into seclusion. During that time she read her Bible and prayed. She said:

> My constant friend was Jesus. One day I knew I had to confront the music room that had me in the grips of severe depression. I had a vivid impression of walking into that room, with Jesus by my side. His arms were wrapped around me. I saw the room, and I was wearing a dress of pure white satin, virginal in appearance.
>
> Jesus, my Friend, my Good Shepherd, cleansed me of my bitter and tainted memories. It was only then that I was prepared to be the bride of the man I loved.

The stories of Lucinda and Jenny are true, although their names have been changed and the circumstances could be repeated in more sordid detail in thousands of other lives.

I do not believe that most non-Christian counselors, no matter how skilled and sympathetic they may be, have the complete solution to such desperate problems. Jesus is the answer, and as we point to Him, those who are crying for help will find the Shepherd who will lead them out of the valleys of despair.

Sometimes I watch Oprah Winfrey's show. I admire her because she listens. However, sometimes when I see the people on the show and the desperate problems they face, I want to cry out to the screen and say to them, "Turn to God!"

He Promises to Provide Superabundantly

God promises "to do immeasurably more than all we ask or imagine, according to his power that is at work within us" (Ephesians 3:20). We need to believe that He can do even more than what we ask. Paul told the Philippians, "My God will meet all your needs according to his glorious riches in Christ Jesus" (4:19). What a promise this is for the Christian! The supply is inexhaustible.

> *Jesus is the answer,*
> *and as we point to Him,*
> *those who are crying for help*
> *will find the Shepherd*
> *who will lead them*
> *out of the valleys of despair.*

We once had a well dug at our home. We reached one layer of water at a hundred feet and another layer of water at three hundred feet, then another at six hundred feet. We asked the well diggers how much water they thought there was. They said there was no way to compute it, but that it would last forever!

God gives us supplies of His power that will never run out. No matter what my need, He is more than able to meet it.

When Do We Need Him?

I find that I need Christ just as much, and sometimes more, in the times when everything seems to be going right as I do in times of trouble. We make the mistake of thinking that Christ's help is needed only for sickrooms, or in times of overwhelming sorrow and suffering. This is not true. When life is going smoothly, we may begin to think it is entirely due to our own goodness, our own power, our own strength. In our triumphs we may forget that Jesus wants to rejoice with us, as well as to weep with us. He went to the wedding at Cana and celebrated with the guests, as well as to the home of Mary and Martha and wept with them after Lazarus had died.

It has been said, "There are just as many stars in the sky at noon as at midnight, although we cannot see them in the sun's glare."

God Promises to Send His Angels

At times in my life I have felt protected in a supernatural way. We have been promised, "For he will command his angels concerning you to guard you in all your ways" (Psalm 91:11).

We face dangers every day of which we are not even aware. Often God intervenes on our behalf through the use of His angels. The Bible is full of the accounts of angels. Psalm 34:7 teaches us that angels protect us and deliver us: "The angel of the Lord encamps around those who fear him, and he delivers them."

Evidence from the Bible, as well as personal experience, convinces us that guardian angels surround us at times and protect us. Many Christians can remember when a near car wreck, a severe accident, or a fierce temptation was averted in some unusual manner. Angels may bring unexpected blessings, like a check in the mail for the exact amount needed, or some food on the doorstep when the cupboards are empty.

"

Whether or not we sense and feel
the presence of the Holy Spirit
or one of the holy angels,
by faith we are certain
God will never leave us nor forsake us.

"

Once when I was going through a dark period I prayed long and earnestly, but there was no answer. I felt as though God was indifferent and that I was all alone with my problem. It was what some would call "a dark night of the soul." I wrote my mother about the experience, and I will never forget her reply: "Son, there are many times when God withdraws to test your faith. He wants you to trust Him in the darkness. Now, Son, reach up by faith in the fog and you will find that His hand will be there." Relieved, I knelt by my bed and experienced an overwhelming sense of God's presence. Whether or not we sense and feel the presence of the Holy Spirit or one of the holy angels, by faith we are certain God will never leave us nor forsake us.

He Walks with Us Through the Fire

When the three Hebrews were thrown into the fire, they didn't know they were going to come out unscathed. They only trusted God that whatever happened to them, it was His will for their lives.

Incredible as it may seem, God wants our companionship; He wants to be close to us. Unlike friends on earth, who may leave us when the going gets rough, He wants to shield us, to protect us, and to guide us in our way through life.

The story has been told about a lone survivor of a shipwreck who was marooned on an uninhabited island. He managed to build a hut in which he put everything he had saved from the wreck. He prayed to God for rescue, and anxiously scanned the horizon every day to signal any passing ship.

One day he returned to his hut and to his horror found it in flames and all of his possessions gone. What a tragedy! Shortly after, a ship arrived. "We saw your smoke signal and hurried here," the captain explained. The survivor had only seen his burnt hut, but out of disaster, God worked a blessing. The shipwrecked man fell to his knees to thank God for the fire that caused his rescue.

When we walk through our fires, He will be with us. He will be our "fourth man in the fire."

11

How to Pray Through the Pain

Groanings which cannot be uttered are often prayers which cannot be refused.
Charles Haddon Spurgeon

PRAYER IS AN EMBARRASSMENT TO SOME. To bow in a restaurant and give thanks, to kneel in a place where others might see you, are outward demonstrations of personal faith. But many people consider them public shows of excessive religiosity. The commitment of the Muslims, in this respect, should be a challenge to us.

In the hard times of life, prayer is no longer awkward, but openly displayed. When the Marines returned to Camp Pendleton, California, after their service in the Persian Gulf War, it was reported that as soon as they spilled out of the airplane, fifteen of the servicemen formed a circle and prayed unashamedly.

Prayer is for every moment of our lives, not just for times of suffering or joy. Prayer is really a place; a place where you meet God in genuine conversation.

Have you ever said, "Well, all we can do now is pray"? Instead of beginning with prayer, we sometimes resort to it after all other resources have been used. When we come to the end of ourselves, we come to the beginning of God. We don't need to be embarrassed that we are needy. God doesn't demand that we pray in King James English, or even with eloquence. Every feeble, stumbling prayer uttered by a believer is heard by God. A cry, a sigh, a "Help!" are all prayers, according to the Psalms.

Frank Laubach, my old friend and a great humanitarian missionary, said, "Prayer at its highest is a two-way conversation—and for me the most important is listening to God's replies." "The polite part of speaking," Edward Gloeggler said, "is to be still long enough to listen."

Many people pray only when they are under great stress or in danger. I have been in airplanes when an engine died; believe me, you could see people praying. I have talked to soldiers who told me that they never prayed until they were in the midst of battle. There seems to be an instinct in man to pray in times of danger. If we are to depend on prayer during tough times, we should be people of prayer before the crisis hits.

Amy Carmichael wrote, "We must learn to pray far more for spiritual victory than for protection from battle-wounds, relief from their havoc, rest from their pain. . . . This triumph is not deliverance from, but victory in trial, and that not intermittent but perpetual."[1]

Our Prayer Model

Jesus is the supreme model of a person devoted to prayer. He was constantly in an attitude of prayer, and never more urgently than in the face of suffering. One of the most amazing things in all the Scriptures is how much time Jesus spent in prayer. He had only three years of public ministry, but He was never too hurried to spend hours in prayer. He prayed before every difficult task and at every crisis in His ministry. No day began or closed in which He was not in communion with His Father.

When He was arrested in the Garden of Gethsemane, He was praying. He had taken the disciples with Him, and sensing the magnitude of what was ahead, He asked Peter, James, and John to stay with Him and keep watch. He went into the garden and fell with His face to the ground, praying, "My Father, if it is possible, may this cup be taken from me. Yet not as I will, but as you will" (Matthew 26:39).

"

No matter how dark and hopeless a situation might seem, never stop praying.

"

We pray so haphazardly. Snatches of memorized verses are hastily spoken in the morning. Then we say good-bye to God for the rest of the day, until we sleepily push through a few closing petitions at night, like leaving a wake-up call at the hotel switchboard. That is not the example of prayer that Jesus gave. He prayed long and repeatedly. He spent at least one entire night in prayer (Luke 6:12).

He prayed briefly when He was in a crowd; He prayed a little longer when He was with His disciples; and He prayed all night when He was alone. Today, many in the ministry tend to reverse that process.

The Scriptures say, "Pray without ceasing" (1 Thessalonians 5:17 KJV). This should be the motto of every true follower of Jesus. No matter how dark and hopeless a situation might seem, never stop praying. It's not only to resolve our problems that we should pray, but to share in the strength of God's friendship. For us, prayer should be not merely an act, but an attitude of life.

Do we pray for God's will, or demand our own way? Prayer needs to be an integral part of our lives, so that when a crisis comes we have the strength and faith to pray for God's will. Someone said that strength in prayer is better than length in prayer. However, Martin Luther said, "I have so much to do today that I shall spend the first three hours in prayer."

A Friend Who Cares

Years ago a student was killed in a fraternity hazing accident at a southern university. John, the star football player at the school, was returning to his dorm on the morning after the tragedy when he saw three athletes mercilessly confront one of the dead boy's friends. That friend later recalled:

> I wanted to make my classes that day, and I was about to break down crying from the taunts of my fellow classmen. I felt like a ten-year-old kid surrounded by high school bullies. I don't think those guys realized what they were doing, but they had me boxed in and they weren't going to let me pass until I broke. One said that at least they didn't kill their pledges! My friend was dead, and these guys wanted to put the blame for his death on me.
>
> Suddenly, there was a hand on my shoulder. It was John. He stood there while I told the story of what had happened, and faced their critical and derisive response. John squeezed my shoulder and gently pushed me on past them.
>
> He walked clear across the campus with me to class. Though we had no classes together, he quietly checked on me during the rest of the day. Perhaps I could have made it through the day, without John, but his being there not only made it easier, but also helped shape my understanding of Christian ministry for the last twenty-two years. John was there when everyone else seemed against me.

Not to share fellowship with Jesus through prayer is sadder than it would have been for that young man to turn to

John, his strong and ready friend, and reject him in that painful time. Not unlike that student, when we turn in prayer to our friend Jesus in time of crisis, sometimes our lives are strengthened forever. In the midst of our trials, He is quietly checking on us.

Pattern for Prayer

Jesus frequently prayed alone, separating Himself from every earthly distraction. I would strongly urge you to select a place—a room or corner in your home, place of work, or in your yard or garden—where you can regularly meet God alone. This does not contradict "Pray without ceasing" (1 Thessalonians 5:17), but expands it.

Jesus prayed with great earnestness. At Gethsemane, in the earnestness of His praying, He fell to the ground and agonized with God until His sweat became "like drops of blood" (Luke 22:44). The force of His prayers was increased during times of extreme suffering.

When we see the need of someone else, pray. When we know someone is in pain, pray. Let someone know you have prayed for them, and ask others to pray for you.

A missionary and his family were forced to camp outside on a hill. They had money with them and were fearful of an attack by roving thieves. After praying, they went to sleep. Months later an injured man was brought into the mission hospital. He asked the missionary if he had soldiers guarding him on that special night. "We intended to rob you," he said, "but we were afraid of the twenty-seven soldiers."

When the missionary returned to his homeland, he related this strange story, and a member of his church said, "We had a prayer meeting that night, and I took the roll. There were just twenty-seven of us present." Prayers have no boundaries. They can leap miles and continents and be translated instantly into any language.

So we not only pray through our pain, but for others as well. Some years ago, the writer and social critic, Tom Wolfe, coined the phrase the "Me Generation." Each generation tends to be a "me" generation, since selfishness is part of human nature. A child says, "It's mine." A teenager centers on his problems. An adult proclaims, "Look out for Number One." Selfishness is part of human nature, but today advertising and "pop" psychology may have raised self-centeredness to state-of-the-art levels. Jesus, on the other hand, tells us to pray not only for ourselves, but even "for those who persecute you" (Matthew 5:44).

We are to plead for our enemies, asking God to lead them to Christ and for His sake to forgive them. Persecution, whether it is physical, social, or mental, is one of the worst types of pain, but those who persecute us are to be the objects of our prayers.

The daughter and son-in-law of Doug Sparks were killed by a drunk driver, and their little boy was injured so badly that his brain will never function normally. A friend said to him after the accident, "Doug, it's going to work out for good for you and your family."

Sparks answered angrily, "Yes, but at what price?"

Sparks said, "For several days I wrestled with the price. I was angry. There's nothing wrong with being angry when something like this strikes you. You just need to stay in contact with God and deal with your anger."

In a time of prayer, it seemed to Sparks that God was saying, "Doug, I know how much this is costing you. I know the price you're paying. But I also know the price I paid."

Sparks continued, "In times of tragedy we must always look to the Cross; the price God paid for a suffering, dying world. Immediately the Spirit witnessed to me that I must go to the driver who had caused the tragedy and forgive him."[2]

He visited the hospital where the driver, an illegal alien, lay strapped down with a broken neck and back and a spirit that was broken even more, sure that God had forsaken him. Sparks shared the Gospel with him and told him, "Because Christ loved me and forgave me, I love you and forgive you." At that moment, Sparks said he experienced the love of Christ for this man. Ordinary human love could not cause that kind of forgiveness for a man who had killed your loved ones, only the prayers of forgiveness could accomplish that miracle.

In His first words uttered from the cross after the nails had been hammered through His hands and feet, Jesus said, "Father, forgive them, for they do not know what they are doing" (Luke 23:34). I have often thought that because of His prayer we will see the men who nailed Jesus to the cross in Heaven. No prayer that Jesus ever prayed to the Father went unanswered.

Christian teachers through the ages have urged the importance of prayer in the lives of believers. One wise man said, "If Christians spent as much time praying as they do grumbling, they would soon have nothing to grumble about."

Someone said, "If there are any tears in Heaven, they will be over the fact that we prayed so little." Cameron Thompson said, "Heaven must be full of answers for which no one ever bothered to ask."[3]

The Power of Prayer

Few of us have learned how to develop the power of prayer. We have not yet learned that a man has more strength when he is at prayer than when he is in control of the most powerful military weapons ever developed. I was pleased to hear General Norman Schwarzkopf in an interview with Barbara Walters after the end of the Gulf War say that he prayed for the men in his command.

Effective prayer is offered in faith. From one end of the Bible to the other, we find the record of people whose prayers have been answered—people who turned the tide of history by prayer, men who prayed fervently and whom God answered.

David gave some powerful prayer patterns in his Psalms for those who are going through difficult times.

When you are distressed: "Answer me when I call to you, O my righteous God, *Give me relief from my distress;* be merciful to me and hear my prayer" (Psalm 4:1, emphasis added).

When you need mercy: "The Lord has heard my cry for *mercy;* the Lord accepts my prayer" (Psalm 6:9, emphasis added).

When you need help: "O Lord my God, I called to you for *help* and you healed me!" (Psalm 30:2, emphasis added).

Prayer is powerful, but if our prayers are aimless, meaningless, and mingled with doubt, they will be of little hope to us. Prayer is more than a wish; it is the voice of faith directed to God. One of my favorite verses is: "If any of you lacks wisdom, he should ask God, who gives generously to all without finding fault, and it will be given to him. But when he asks, he must believe and not doubt, because he who doubts is like a wave of the sea, blown and tossed by the wind" (James 1:5–6).

The Bible says, "The prayer of a righteous man is powerful and effective" (James 5:16). Jesus said, "I tell you, whatever you ask for in prayer, believe that you have received it, and it will be yours" (Mark 11:24). I have heard many stories of prayers being answered for a loved one miles way. One mother told about a time when she clearly heard one of her daughters cry, "Mom, Mom!" in the middle of the night. But her daughter was a married woman, traveling halfway around the world with her husband. The mother picked up her Bible from the nightstand and went into the family room to pray. She had a real sense of urgency that her daughter needed help. She prayed that God would show her what to do, and then she read Psalm 91 over and over again.

A few weeks later she received a letter from her daughter. This is what had happened. The daughter was in Borneo when she became very sick and feverish. Her husband could not find a good doctor, but after some time located one who took them into his home where he and his housekeeper nursed the woman back to health. The letter ended, "Remember when I was a girl and I would call out, 'Mom,' and you would come rushing down the hall? That night in Borneo, in my fever, I called, 'Mom, Mom' . . . and then I could hear you rushing down the hall."[4]

God sometimes causes us pain so that we may pray for others. Bible teaching, church history, and Christian experience all confirm that prayer does work.

Pray, Don't Panic

When we're in a threatening situation, the normal tendency is to panic. Many stories could be told of fear being replaced by calm through the power of prayer.

Carol is a victim of multiple sclerosis, which is a disease of the central nervous system. Everyone has different symptoms of MS, some more debilitating than others. Over the years this once active and vibrant woman gradually lost a great deal of her muscular ability and was confined to a wheelchair.

Her husband always saw that she was comfortably situated before leaving for work. Being a methodical man, he was used to returning home at a certain time each afternoon.

One day Carol was attempting to get from her wheelchair into her bed, and somehow she fell and her head became wedged between the wall and the wheels of her chair. She was trapped and couldn't move to reach the phone. She began to pray for help, knowing that the longer she lay on the cold, hard floor, the more difficult it would be to regain any muscular strength. Only a short time passed before she heard the door open and her husband calling to her. He had arrived hours before his normal time.

"I seemed to have someone telling me to come home," he told his wife as he lifted her into bed.

Carol said, "And I know who that Someone was. I prayed for help."

Our prayers are not always answered as quickly and specifically as Carol's. If we remain calm, placing faith in God and believing that we will receive God's direction, we will eventually find the answer to our problem.

Creative Silence

The story is told about Robert LeTourneau, the industrialist, who received an order from the government for a very complicated machine to be used in lifting airplanes. No machine of this type had ever been designed. LeTourneau and his engineers could not come up with a plan. After some time everyone was becoming tense and nervous. Finally, on a Wednesday night, LeTourneau told his staff that he was not going to work, that he was going to a prayer meeting. The engineers were upset, because they had a deadline and the boss was deserting them.

"But," he said, "I've got a deadline with God." He went to the prayer meeting, sang the hymns, and prayed. Afterward, as he was walking home, the design of the machine in complete detail came into his mind. He needed time with God and creative silence to bring it to the surface.[5]

Sometimes we try so hard to solve the problems of our health, our children, our business, or our future that we become agitated or depressed. "Be still, and know that I am God" (Psalm 46:10).

Prayer Is a Place in Your Heart

Prayer is more than a plea, it is a place where we must spend time if we are to learn its power.

A minister had gradually lost his faith. In a world of great suffering, he could no longer feel the presence of the Lord in his own life. He was embittered that he had spent so much of his life in studying and pursuing an understanding of God. Now he had only a sense of betrayal and emptiness. Even his prayers seemed to bounce off an invisible barrier.

He expressed his anguish to an old friend he had known since his childhood. He told his friend that he thought he knew what Moses would have felt like if the burning bush had suddenly stopped burning and went up in a pale, gritty puff of smoke. He said that for him there was no more burning bush or sense of the presence of God in his life.

His friend, a rancher, confided that he, too, often felt that way. "But you know, Jack, I realized a while back that the burning bush is always there, always burning. It's just that I hadn't been spending much time in that part of the pasture."

Prayer is "that part of the pasture" where the bush is burning. If we are to be powerful in prayer, we must spend time there.

Thy Will Be Done

As we face problems and personal suffering, we must not forget that our prayers are subject to His will. This takes the burden off of us and gives it to the Lord. His will is always best. The difficulty most of us face is knowing the will of God. As believers, we cannot find true peace outside the will of God.

In our computerized society, many people have learned the value of using these amazing machines. A computer, however, has no worth unless it is programmed. When the proper data is put into it, it will do more work accurately than many people. The believer has tremendous potential, but that potential cannot be used until he is programmed with the Word of God.

J. Grant Howard said: "God has given every believer a handbook with many of the basic rules and regulations for life. If and when a believer follows these rules, he is in the will of God. When he consciously violates them, he is out of the will of God. Therefore I must know the precepts taught in the Word if I am going to do the will of God."[6]

"

God is true to His word and answers all sincere prayers offered in the name of the Lord Jesus Christ.

"

Prayers that are selfish, vengeful, or mean are not in the will of God. However, we may be sure that God is true to His word and answers all sincere prayers offered in the name of the Lord Jesus Christ. His answer may be yes, or it may be no, or it may be "Wait." If it is no or "Wait," we cannot say that God has not answered our prayer. It simply means that the answer is different from what we expected.

When we pray for help in trouble, or for healing in sickness, or for deliverance in persecution, God may not give us what we ask for because that may not be His wise and loving will for us. He will answer our prayer in His own way, and He will not let us down in our hour of need.

Margaret Clarkson said, "It's not wrong to pray for miracles. But it is wrong to insist upon our own will rather than God's. We may not demand miracles of a sovereign God.

Unfortunately, such demands are made in all too many Christian circles today."[7]

True prayer is a way of life, not just for use in cases of emergency. Make it a habit, and when the need arises you will be in practice.

12

Storing Up for the Storms

You cannot suddenly fabricate foundations of strength; they must have been building all along.

Philip Yancey

TOM LANDRY, FORMER COACH OF THE Dallas Cowboys, has spoken at our Crusades and is a man I greatly admire. Because he was well known to many, his Christian testimony influenced thousands, particularly when it was known that he was in a tight spot.

Landry did not become a Christian until he was thirty-three years old, even though he had been a churchgoer all his life. One of his biographers wrote: "There would be shaky times, frustrating times that would follow, some of which would have deeply scarred those with less faith. But Landry's faith would help sustain him. It is doubtful he would have gotten through the ordeal of being fired when he was looking forward to trying to bring the team back if his faith had not been so strong. It is also doubtful he would have gotten through the Dallas Cowboy's formative years, which were much worse than he could have imagined."[1]

What guides a man like Tom Landry, giving him the resources to store up for the storms in life? Repeatedly, we hear the word "faith." Faith in Jesus Christ.

An athlete does not try out for the Olympics without hours and hours, years and years of training. An actor doesn't go onstage without memorizing his lines. A cook can't bake a cake without the necessary ingredients. Why, then, do we expect to meet life and its painful twists without the strengthening resources we need?

What Would You Do?

What would you do if the major cities in your country were suddenly leveled by guided missiles or enemy bombers? How would you react if an earthquake cut off all communication, water, and electrical sources? Suppose a group of terrorists kept you hostage? If you have never experienced such extreme horrors, you probably have no answers.

We should not live our lives anticipating disasters. I have known people who build up such fears for what might happen that they never enjoy what is happening. However, like national defense, we need to arm ourselves. George Washington said, "To be prepared for war is one of the most effectual means of preserving peace."

However, we in America, in comparison with Christians in many other countries, have experienced very little sacrifice and suffering. I know of the plight of the homeless and the poor and am not insensitive to their needs. For most of us, any persecution we may have undergone has been minor.

Christianity in America has at times become almost popular. Walk into any Christian bookstore and see the hundreds of books that are published. Well-known people openly profess their Christian belief. However, I believe that as secular materialism becomes increasingly prevalent in our educational system, the time of popularity will soon come to an end. Already we are experiencing the curtailment of prayer and Bible study. And our young people are paying the price. Christ warned His followers that to believe in Him would not make them popular, and that they should be prepared to face affliction for His sake.

Will We Escape Religious Persecution?

Some anti-abortion groups have been put in jail, some have been mistreated. In our schools, parents who have opposed objectionable material in the classroom have been called extremists or worse. Can we compare these with the persecutions in countries where Christians have been jailed, tortured, or killed?

> *“Already we are experiencing the curtailment of prayer and Bible study. And our young people are paying the price.”*

The Bible says that all who want “to live a godly life in Christ Jesus will be persecuted” (2 Timothy 3:12). Jesus said that as the time of His return comes closer, “They will lay hands on you and persecute you” (Luke 21:12).

The fact that we are not being persecuted for Christ’s sake is an abnormal situation. I am not suggesting America is about to undergo torture for Christ, but even subtle persecution for our faith is likely to cause many believers to deny Him.

Are we too soft, too used to the luxuries of freedom, that we would be unable to stand up to persecution? Most of us would do no more, no less, than we are doing right now. Some of us who wear our Christianity on our sleeves would probably be the first to surrender. Many would be modern-day Peters who would say, “Though all others deny Christ, yet I will never deny him.” But he did. Three times.

Others, depending on Christ's strength and power, would be strong and courageous. They would find their strength, as the Apostle Paul did, in Christ's promise, "My power is made perfect in weakness" (2 Corinthians 12:9).

Persecutions of the Heart

Claudia was a newlywed in her twenties when she was diagnosed with Hodgkin's disease and was given only a 50 percent chance of survival. Rapidly she was operated on and began cobalt treatments that transformed her almost overnight from a young, beautiful woman to a wreck.

Her Christian friends came with confusing, not consoling, words of help. All the comforters with their conflicting voices only added to her misery. Her husband was a chaplain's assistant in a hospital and had seen many sides of suffering. He said, "I had seen sick and dying patients. In the movies, couples who have fought for years, suddenly in the face of danger forget their differences and come together. But it doesn't work that way in real life.

"When a couple encounters a crisis," he said, "it magnifies what's already present in the relationship. Since Claudia and I happened to love each other deeply, and had worked on open communication, the crisis drove us to each other. Feelings of blame and anger against each other did not creep in. The crisis of her illness merely brought to the surface and intensified feelings already present."[2]

Problems magnify what is already present in our relationship with those close to us. Claudia and her husband may not have realized that they were prepared for this crisis in their life, but their solid love bonded them as a fortress to meet the storm. Fortunately, Claudia was eventually cured by treatments that destroyed the cancerous cells.

Other couples and families are driven apart by troubles. Like a tree with shallow roots, they are flattened when the winds come. Some get divorces, some have family splits that never seem to heal. Accusations, bitterness, hatred, and guilt destroy relationships that should have grown stronger like a healthy tree.

If we want to have resources in our possession for a day of disaster, each one of us must have a personal survival kit.

God's Storehouse

Before Easter many of the television channels showed the film classic *The Ten Commandments.* There is one scene where Moses opens Pharaoh's grain house and the starving Jews swarm in with their baskets and fill them from the steady stream of life-giving grain that poured out of giant bins.

"*Getting to know God and being able to call on Him is the most important step in storing up for the storms.*"

God has just such a storehouse of supplies. But there are some requirements for us to meet before we can receive the abundance. First, we must make sure of our relationship to God. We must be prepared to meet God at any moment.

Isn't it strange how we prepare for so many things except meeting God? Some girls spend months preparing for their wedding, down to the details of how many layers on the cake and what flavor. Do they prepare for the life after the wedding?

Getting to know God and being able to call on Him is the most important step in storing up for the storms.

Knowing God is more than just treating Him as a casual acquaintance, but developing a deeper relationship with Him every day.

Second, we should learn how to walk with God in our daily life. Have you ever been asked, "How is your walk?" Some Christians will know immediately that you are asking about their walk with God, but many will probably say, "Well, I do about two miles a day."

I know people who seem to be holding the hand of God throughout their life's journey. I also know people who are lagging far behind. We have some friends in the Old Testament who have given us vivid examples of walking with God.

Abraham walked with God and was called a friend of God. Noah walked with God, and when the flood came he was saved. Moses walked with God in the desert, and when the hour of judgment fell upon Egypt, he was prepared to lead his people to victory. David walked with God as a shepherd boy, and when he was called upon to rule his people, he was prepared for the task of being a king. Daniel was saved from the lions' den, and his friends were spared from the fiery furnace.

God does not always pull his children out of deep water. Stephen was a young man "full of faith and of the Holy Spirit" (Acts 6:5). He was stoned to death, but his entry into Heaven was triumphal.

Wouldn't you think that the apostles would have fared better than some of the scoundrels that surrounded Jesus? Just look at some of their fates: Peter was crucified upside down; Andrew was tied to a cross with thick ropes for three days before he died; John was a prisoner on a desolate island; Bartholomew was beaten and then beheaded; Thomas was murdered while he was preaching. Amy Carmichael said, "For John, the beloved disciple, was reserved the long martyrdom of life."

These men literally walked with God. Although we were not present two thousand years ago, we have access to the same strength as the apostles.

Take Your Bible off the Shelf

What has happened to Bible memorization? Children in Sunday school used to have verses to memorize in order to win a Bible. Bible studies used to have passages to commit to memory. Today there are more people who know the words to a television commercial than know the words in the Bible.

Many stories have come out of prison camps about Christians who had no Bibles but who had committed portions of the Scripture to memory and shared them with others. One Christian who was in a prison camp for three years told me that during his imprisonment his greatest regret was not having memorized more of the Bible.

A Chinese missionary was imprisoned by the Japanese during World War II. She managed to take a forbidden Gospel of John with her. When she went to bed, she pulled the covers over her head, and memorized one verse each night for three years.

When the prisoners were released, most of them shuffled out, but the missionary was so chipper that someone said she must have been brainwashed. A *Life* magazine reporter, who had interviewed her, said, "She's been brainwashed for sure. God washed her brain."

People have told me that when they were suffering that sometimes they could only remember small parts of Scripture. One woman, upon hearing bad news, repeated over and over again, "I can do everything through him who gives me strength" (Philippians 4:13).

What verses have you stored up for the future?

Be a Prayer Warrior Before the Battle Begins

We have talked about the importance of prayer before, but it seems as if we pray during a crisis and neglect it in-between. In the weeks since the end of the war in the Persian Gulf, I have heard or read very little about prayers for our country. On the other hand, we have so many battles going on in America today that we should be a people of prayer. Our government needs prayer. Our leaders need prayer. Our schools need prayer. Our youth need our prayers. Our families need our prayers.

If Christianity is to survive in a godless and materialistic world, we must repent of our prayerlessness. We must make prayer our priority. Even our churches today have gotten away from prayer meetings. Potlucks and fund raising seem to have taken precedence.

Are we spiritually prepared as individuals or as a nation for the increasing attacks upon us? I believe in military preparation, but it cannot take the place of spiritual preparedness.

We do not have wicked men at the head of our government. In fact, many of them are godly people, devoted to their families and to the protection of our nation. However, we do have "spiritual forces of evil" at work in our world. The daily news tells us of increasing depravity every year. We must be prayer warriors against these "powers of darkness."

A story about the weapon of prayer being used against a wicked ruler is told in the Bible. Sennacherib was an Assyrian leader who had boasted that he would defeat God's people and take over their land. His propaganda machine was powerful. He sent messages to Israel, taunting the people about their weakness and boasting of his strength. In the arms race of their day, the Assyrians were definitely ahead. When Sennacherib spoke, the whole world trembled!

Israel's king, Hezekiah, was a man of faith. He knew that on a purely human level the Assyrians could destroy them. But Hezekiah had a secret weapon. He called the prophet Isaiah in, and they fell to their knees in prayer.

Look what happened: "And the Lord sent an angel, who annihilated all the fighting men and the leaders and officers in the camp of the Assyrian king. So he [Sennacherib] withdrew to his own land in disgrace. . . . So the Lord saved Hezekiah and the people of Jerusalem. . . . He took care of them on every side" (2 Chronicles 32:21–22).

> *We have so many battles going on in America today that we should be a people of prayer.*

Miracles have happened when God's people turned to Him in prayer. We should not pray for God to be on our side, but pray that we may be on God's side. God does not always deliver His children out of a catastrophe, but promises to be with us throughout.

Practice the Presence of Christ

How do we experience the nearness of the Lord at all times? Do we need a picture drawn by some creative artist to be able to imagine Him with us? Charles Spurgeon once said that there had never been fifteen minutes in his life when he did not sense the presence of Christ. I wish I could make that statement, but I regret that I cannot. What strength we would have, not only during days of testing and suffering, if we trained for life with Christ walking alongside of us.

In His Steps was a bestseller that told of a challenge given by a pastor to his people to pledge for one year not to do anything without first asking the question, "What would Jesus do?" This challenge was provoked when a shabby man, mourning his wife who had died in poverty, stumbled into this wealthy church and addressed the congregation. He said,

> I heard some people singing at a church prayer meeting the other night,
>
> All for Jesus, all for Jesus;
> All my being's ransomed powers;
> All my thoughts and all my doings,
> All my days and all my hours;
>
> I kept wondering as I sat on the steps outside just what they meant by it. It seems to me there's an awful lot of trouble in the world that somehow wouldn't exist if all the people who sing such songs went and lived them out.[3]

If that tramp had posed the same question to us, what would be our response? Do we live our lives with the thought, "What would Jesus do?" Do we practice the presence of Christ every day?

In the story, the tramp died, but he struck the conscience of the minister so profoundly that the lives of many people in the town were changed, just as our lives would change if we truly followed "in His steps" and asked, "What would Jesus have me do?"

Christ promised His disciples, "And surely I will be with you always, to the very end of the age" (Matthew 28:20). What great reassurance that is! The fact of His presence is there because He promised. We need to cultivate the sense of His presence, as we go about the daily routine of our lives.

Christ must be vitally real to us if we are to remain faithful to Him in the hour of crisis. Who knows when that hour might be? Things are happening so fast that the need for turning to God has never been more urgent.

I have told this story many times, and I ask my wife to forgive me for repeating it again. However, it is such a great example of "storing up for the storms," that I cannot leave it out.

Several years ago Ruth had a terrible fall and suffered a concussion. She was unconscious for nearly a week, broke her foot in five places, broke a rib, cracked a vertebra, and injured her hip. Some of those injuries have lingered with her. When she regained consciousness, she found she had lost a great deal of her memory. Most disturbing to her was that she had forgotten all of the Scriptures she had learned throughout the years. The verses of a lifetime were more precious to her than any of her material possessions.

"

What would Jesus do?

"

One night when she was praying, she said, "Lord, take anything I have, but please bring back my Bible verses."

Immediately this verse came to mind, "I have loved thee with an everlasting love: therefore with lovingkindness have I drawn thee." Strangely, she did not remember memorizing that verse, but the Lord brought it back to her.

She has continued to memorize, although she finds as she gets older that it takes longer. One of the most recent passages has been Romans 8:31–39.

I want to include this passage here, urging you to memorize it and hide it away in your heart. When persecution, trouble, and adversity arise, these verses will come back to you and give you hope and strength.

> What, then, shall we say in response to this? If God is for us, who can be against us? He who did not spare his own Son, but gave him up for us all—how will he not also, along with him, graciously give us all things? Who will bring any charge against those whom God has chosen? It is God who justifies. Who is he that condemns? Christ Jesus, who died—more than that, who was raised to life—is at the right hand of God and is also interceding for us. Who shall separate us from the love of Christ? Shall trouble or hardship or persecution or famine or nakedness or danger or sword? As it is written:
>
> "For your sake we face death all day long;
> we are considered as sheep to be slaughtered."
>
> No, in all these things we are more than conquerors through him who loved us. For I am convinced that neither death nor life, neither angels nor demons, neither the present nor the future, nor any powers, neither height nor depth, nor anything else in all creation, will be able to separate us from the love of God that is in Christ Jesus our Lord.

What a great storehouse we will have when those thoughts are in our hearts!

Family Power

A few years ago I had not heard the term "dysfunctional family" used as it is today. Now the concept is applied to so many that I begin to wonder how the family is functioning. In most parts of the world, it is not operating too well. I am not speaking only of the immediate family unit, but of the extended family and also the family of God. There is no need to review all the problems. You know them. In fact, you may be a part of the problem. Only the strong Christian family unit can survive the increasing world crises.

The previous points in our discussion of the storehouse apply to the family also. First, we need to place God at the center of our family. Second, as a family we need to walk with God daily. Third, consulting and memorizing Scripture as a family is vital. Together the family should read, mark, and learn the Scriptures as an essential preparation for the persecution ahead.

> "*Only the strong Christian family unit can survive the increasing world crises.*"

Family prayer is a fourth vital link in the chain of spiritual strength—a strength we are trying to build to protect us from a world gone mad. Practicing prayer as a family, not just a flippant blessing before a meal, can give us the security we need.

If a family is fragmented, divided into factions or unforgiving in its attitude toward its members, it will have painful times when trouble hits. Many times it takes just one member of a family to initiate the action to bring a family back together again.

One couple we know was remarried after their son finally approached his father and said, "I think you and Mother ought to get back together again." At the ceremony, the boy took a quantity of Kleenex, thinking his mother would need it, but it was the father to whom he had to keep passing the tissues as he stood with tears streaming down his face. Through the intervention of a child, the years of hurt, pain, and fragmentation of that broken family were brought to an end with a new beginning.

Family includes those small, intimate groups that are springing up inside and outside the church today. In an impersonal society, where often we don't know our next-door neighbor, there is a basic need for support groups. Many people don't have it within their family. When brothers and sisters in Christ unite in a home Bible class or a study group, their faith and witness can be strengthened. Scripture urges us to "Bear ye one another's burdens, and so fulfil the law of Christ" (Galatians 6:2 KJV). When this is done in small Christian groups, amazing things can happen.

One group of Christian business people met to pray for a friend who had suffered a severe stroke. Gradually, the prayer group became a true support group, where they openly shared their feelings and read the Scriptures together. The man who had had the stroke came to thank them for their prayers and stayed to accept Christ. Soon his wife came to a potluck they were having, and she eventually was born again. Amazing things can happen when the family of God bands together.

Ruth and I have learned that the church in China has survived after many years of severe restrictions. How could this be? It is because of small groups of believers, who, though often driven "underground" during the Cultural Revolution, managed to meet regularly around the Word. Despite the concerted effort to destroy all the Bibles in China, some copies survived. Small groups of Christians met around these and were also nurtured by the verses memorized by other believers. Chinese Christians in prisons and labor camps have allowed the flame of their faith to burn brightly and have been used to lead other Chinese to the Lord. Consequently, the number of Christians has multiplied under persecution.

What about us? Are we preparing for the storms of suffering, or will we be caught without resources? The best way to prepare is to deepen our spiritual lives—and by that I mean to deepen our life in the Spirit.

Being filled with the Spirit is not a one-time affair but an ongoing experience. When Paul said, "Be filled with the Spirit" (Ephesians 5:18), he conveyed the idea that we "keep on being filled with the Spirit." This is not a pond of water, but an ever-flowing spring. We are to have these storehouses that are available for our use at all times. When the resources are needed, they will be there.

So be prepared. When the "evil day" comes, we do not have to be dependent upon the circumstances around us, but rather on the resources of God!

13

How to Help the Hurting People

In order to console, there is no need to say much. It is enough to listen, to understand, to love.

Paul Tournier

AN ANCIENT PHILOSOPHER, WHO WAS the wisest man of his time, wrote: "Two are better than one, because they have a good return for their work: If one falls down, his friend can help him up. But pity the man who falls and has no one to help him up" (Ecclesiastes 4:9–10).

Hurting people are lonely people. It may seem like the whole world goes on, and nobody cares. It has been said that loneliness is the disease of our time. Loneliness lingers in the hospital bed and sits with the wife whose husband spends more time at work than at home. Loneliness strikes the divorced husband or wife and the children who are left behind. Loneliness isolates the aged and impersonalizes the poor. Cities are often the loneliest places in the world.

David Jeremiah wrote: "What is loneliness? Some describe it in physical terms. It's an empty feeling in the pit of one's stomach, almost to the point of nausea. Others describe it as an underlying anxiety, 'a big black pit.' Some say loneliness is a sharp ache in moments of grief or separation. For others it's a long period of stress that wears them down until they're discouraged and defeated."[1]

Lonely people, hurting people need someone to help them up. To encourage them, to support them, to let them know they're not alone. Who are the helpers, the comforters for the times when we're bleeding and need a transfusion of love?

We can talk about God being our Comforter, but that doesn't absolve us of our responsibility. He has given us a special assignment. The Apostle Paul said: "Praise be to the God and Father of our Lord Jesus Christ, the Father of compassion and the God of all comfort, who comforts us in all our troubles, so that we can comfort those in any trouble with the comfort we ourselves have received from God" (2 Corinthians 1:3–4).

We don't have to be psychologists or trained counselors or ministers to be comforters. At some time we are all called to be comforters. Even a child can comfort with a pat or a dog with a lick.

Are We Approachable?

Does someone who is hurting feel free to tell us their problem, to cry on our shoulders, if necessary, or to ask for help? Or do we change the subject, tell a joke, or quote a Bible verse to make everything better?

Teri was a young bride when she invited Phyllis, an older Christian career woman, to have lunch. Teri was very disturbed and needed help. Phyllis, on the other hand, was someone who faced many problems every day in her business and brushed them off with positive affirmations. Instead of being open to Teri, she replied with all of the clichés, such as, "Just turn a lemon into lemonade," or "Let's look at the bright side." There's nothing wrong with those concepts, except that Teri needed someone to help her up, not give her platitudes that made her feel guilty for being discouraged.

If people feel safe disclosing their problems to us, most likely we are approachable. Confidentiality is the essence of being trusted. If our non-Christian friends don't feel that they can trust us with their hurts, we may never be able to approach them with their need for Jesus Christ.

Are You Available?

"When I lost my husband, I saw people I had known for years pretend not to see me in the market, or walk on the other side of the street if they saw me coming. I felt like a leper." This is how a woman described her feeling of isolation when she needed conversation and comfort. Deliberate avoidance is practiced when we don't know what to say. It is an insensitive attitude toward a hurting person. Don't be afraid to approach a person in pain. If he or she doesn't want to talk about it, you'll know. Chances are, they want someone to listen. Inside, they may be like the Psalmist who cried, "Turn to me and be gracious to me, for I am lonely and afflicted" (Psalm 25:16).

> "*Confidentiality is the essence of being trusted.*"

Being available is difficult, because it takes time, but being sensitive to the small amounts of time we can give could reap large rewards in someone's life. It doesn't really matter what we say to comfort people during a time of suffering, it's our concern and availability that count.

When my wife's father died, her mother was left incapacitated by a stroke, confined to a wheelchair and limited in her speech. Friends and neighbors dropped by to comfort her. Those who comforted the most, said the least. They were widows themselves. All they did was put their arms around her and weep together briefly. But Mother was comforted. One day a group of college students came from the local college. They gathered around her on the floor—wall to wall—and accompanied by a guitar, they sang hymns. That was all.

Philip Yancey tells about a man who said nothing when he heard about a family tragedy, and yet spoke volumes. "A story is told about Beethoven, a man not known for social grace. Because of his deafness, he found conversation difficult and humiliating. When he heard of the death of a friend's son, Beethoven hurried to the house, overcome with grief. He had no words of comfort to offer. But he saw a piano in the room. For the next half hour he played the piano, pouring out his emotions in the most eloquent way he could. When he finished playing, he left. The friend later remarked that no one else's visit had meant so much."[2]

During the Persian Gulf War, Isaac Stern was playing in Tel Aviv with the symphony. Suddenly, sirens began to wail, alerting everyone to an incoming missile attack from Iraq. Afraid of the possibility of a poison gas attack, the government had issued gas masks to everyone. So in the middle of the concert, the people in the audience grabbed their masks and put them on. Everyone wore a mask, except the maestro. One cannot easily forget the picture that flashed across our television screens of Isaac Stern playing his heart out to an audience of faceless masks.

Being available is not a statement, it's an action.

Don't Add to the Hurt

Sometimes instead of helping the hurting, we hinder them. We may hurt others deliberately and sometimes inadvertently. Some churches are accused of "shooting their wounded." This may happen when all the blame for the break-up of a marriage is put upon one member of the couple.

A child may go astray, and the parents are made to feel guilty. A businessman files for bankruptcy, and people begin to question his honesty. There are so many ways we can add to another's hurt.

Tony had taken a bad fall off a roof and broken his neck. For more than a week it was not known whether he would be completely paralyzed or not. He looked terrible as he lay in bed with metal pins through his skull and surrounded by sandbags, his face bruised and swollen. The family feared for their father's recovery and needed loving support themselves.

A daughter said,

> People from the church came to visit and the moment they saw Dad, the shock of his appearance made their stay very brief. They patted me on the shoulder and headed for the door as fast as they could. We had the impression that they came because it was the "thing to do."
>
> But there was one man who was not a Christian. He was a poor immigrant, not eloquent, but a man Dad had talked to about the Lord. He came in the room and simply said, "I know that your God will take care of you." He would look at Dad, pat his hand, and walk out. But he came every day, and always said the same thing. He comforted us, because he shared with us the faith we knew Dad had.

We flourish with kindness and shrivel with unkindness. Few Christians are deliberately unkind, but some do not realize the effect they may have by the look on their faces or the tone of their voices. Someone said, "The nicest thing we can do for our heavenly Father is to be kind to one of His children." How true that is. I know how grateful I am when someone is kind to one of my children.

Gossip is another way in which we hurt others. "May the absent always feel safe with us" is a motto to be remembered. Even in prayer meetings, gossip may be transmitted in the form of prayers.

We add to the hurt when we are critical. Criticism has a withering effect upon people, especially our children. They need guidance and correcting, but constant criticism will destroy their spirit and their ability to succeed.

Dr. James Dobson has probably helped more parents and teachers understand how to bring up their children in the way they should go than anyone in our current society. He wrote in his classic, *Dare to Discipline:* "Too often our parental instruction consists of a million 'don'ts' which are jammed down the child's throat. We should spend more time rewarding him for the behavior we do admire, even if our 'reward' is nothing more than a sincere compliment. Remembering the child's need for self-esteem and acceptance, the wise parent can satisfy those important longings while using them to teach valued concepts and behavior."[3]

In David's prayer for his son Solomon, he said, "Prayer also shall be made for him continually; and daily shall he be praised" (Psalm 72:15 KJV). What a great suggestion for parents! Pray continually and praise daily. Failure to do this will cause more damage than we may be able to repair.

Failure to encourage is one of the commonest ways to hurt other people. There are so many hurts that circumstances and the world inflict upon us, we need the constant reinforcement of encouragement.

My mother was one of my greatest encouragers. In my book *Facing Death,* I said, "Mother always told me to preach the Gospel, and keep it simple. Two weeks before she went to be with the Lord she admonished me with the same words. I said, 'Mother, I'm going to preach His birth, death, and resurrection. I'll preach it until Jesus comes.'

"She squeezed my hand and said, 'I believe it.'

"What a blessing it is for parents to believe in their children."

Another way to hurt people is by being too busy. Too busy to notice their needs. Too busy to drop that note of comfort or encouragement or assurance of love. Too busy to listen when someone needs to talk. Too busy to simply care. When Alan Redpath was pastor at the Moody Church in Chicago, he had this saying on the wall of his study: "Beware of the barrenness of a busy life."

It's amazing how we can hurt others, especially those close to us. We see examples all the time of the subtle and not-so-subtle ways in which wives belittle husbands and vice versa. One incident was related to me about a woman who was constantly berating her husband about being a little overweight. They were having dinner at a home where there were other guests present. The hostess served the dessert, a delectable looking chocolate mousse. The wife looked at it, reached for the salt shaker which had remained on the table, and proceeded to douse her husband's dessert with the salt. "Now you won't be tempted," she announced smugly. I heard later that they had divorced.

"A keen sense of humor helps us to overlook the unbecoming, understand the unconventional, tolerate the unpleasant, overcome the unexpected, and outlast the unbearable."

One incident that greatly amused Ruth in her childhood was the time when two missionaries had to journey through Shanghai and stayed in the "Missionary Home," then run by two English ladies. Dr. Patterson, quite a large woman, was a medical doctor, and her husband was a slight, rather frail man. He was not very well, being allergic to certain foods that his wife knew he should not eat. The lady who ran the Home became increasingly indignant when she noticed that whenever anything particularly good was put before Mr. Patterson, his wife quickly removed it to her plate and ate it. Mr. Patterson had a great sense of humor. He noticed his hostess' growing indignation. One day when the dessert was served, he amused and gratified her as, with eyes twinkling, he gobbled it down before his wife could object, even though he knew it would make him sick and he would pay for it later!

A keen sense of humor helps us to overlook the unbecoming, understand the unconventional, tolerate the unpleasant, overcome the unexpected, and outlast the unbearable.

We never gain in life by hurting others. Sometimes we try to elevate our own insecure egos by degrading and belittling those around us. Yet this produces only a false sense of self-esteem.

The Bible teaches us to be more concerned about the needs and feelings of others than our own. We are to encourage and build self-confidence in our loved ones, friends, and associates. A true servant of God is someone who helps another succeed. "Therefore encourage one another and build each other up" (1 Thessalonians 5:11). Someone said, "You can never speak a fine word too soon, for you never know how soon it will be too late."

Bear One Another's Burdens

Bob Pierce was a man who knew what it was to bear another's burdens. He was one of the most remarkable men I have ever known, a great evangelical humanitarian, cofounder of Youth for Christ, founder of World Vision, and, later in his life, founder of Samaritan's Purse, which is now headed by my son Franklin. I loved and admired this amazing man who was a friend of the "little" people, the forgotten, the hurting people who are unheard of and unsung except in the courts of Heaven.

He once told Franklin, "The only measurement I had in assessing what we should be involved in was 'Is this something Jesus would do? Something God would want done?' Ultimately it boiled down to something I wrote in my Bible on Kojedo Island: 'Let my heart be broken with the things that break the heart of God.'"

> "*It's so easy to give to a charity or a ministry and feel good about it. It's not so easy to provide the personal charity.*"

I remember one story about Dr. Bob Pierce that exemplified the ability to be a bearer of someone's burdens. "Borneo Bob" Williams was a missionary who started hundreds of churches in Kaliminatan, which is now a part of Indonesia. Dr. Bob was dying of leukemia, and, knowing that he only had a short time to live, he went to Kaliminatan to say goodbye to Borneo Bob. Here's the story:

> While he was there (in Kaliminatan), on his way down to the river, he noticed a girl lying on a bamboo mat and asked Bob Williams what she was doing there. Bob Williams explained that she was dying of a form of cancer and had very few days to live. Dr. Bob's anger flared. "How come this girl is lying down there in the mud when she could be up there in that nice, clean clinic?" he stormed.

> Borneo Bob explained that this girl was a jungle girl and preferred to be near the river where it was cooler, that she had specifically asked to be placed there for the day. Bob Pierce's heart broke. He went over to the girl, knelt down beside her, held her hand, and, rubbing her forehead, he prayed for her. After he prayed, she looked up and said something to him. He turned to Borneo Bob, who translated what she had said, explaining that with her disease and the unbearable pain she was unable to sleep and was dying, "If I could only sleep again, if I could only sleep again!" Bob Pierce began to cry, for he himself was dying of leukemia and had less than a year to live, and he knew what it was to be unable to sleep. He reached into his pocket and grabbed his bottle of sleeping pills. He gave it to Bob Williams and said, "You make sure she gets a good night's sleep from now on." Dr. Bob knew that he would have to go another ten days before he could get to Singapore and replace his medication—he knew that he would have to forfeit ten nights of sleep for this little girl.[4]

When the Good Samaritan found a man robbed, beaten, and left for dead, he didn't continue on his trip and "report the accident." He didn't call 911 and leave the scene, nor pay someone else to go back and care for the man. The Samaritan himself got involved.

He tenderly lifted the wounded body onto his own donkey and continued on the journey to Jericho. When he reached the city, he found a place to stay, and probably cared for the patient. The next day, he made arrangements with the innkeeper to pay all financial debts that the patient would incur.

That is what bearing one another's burdens is all about. It's so easy to give to a charity or a ministry and feel good about it. It's not so easy to provide the personal charity. It's easier to give to someone overseas than it is to take a casserole next door.

May God give us the sensitivity to recognize the needs of those around us and lend a helping hand.

Pray for Those Who Hurt

A simple prayer, a Scripture that has meant something to you, these can be a great comfort to a hurting person. The Word of God is where we "find grace to help us in our time of need" (Hebrews 4:16).

Rather than giving personal advice, how much better would it be for Christians to share God's loving promises. It is a comfort to hear the words of God in times of stress. If you have problems remembering proper verses, there are some fine little booklets that you can carry in your pocket or purse which give verses for many different situations.

"

It is a comfort to hear
the words of God
in times of stress.

"

I remember a time in my late teens when I had a case of "puppy love," which was very real to the "puppy." We were even talking about marriage, although we were both much too young. However, she felt the Lord was leading her to another young man who was one of my best friends. I felt like my heart would break, so I went to a clergyman friend of mine for help. He turned to 2 Corinthians 1:3–4, 6. The passage not only tells us we are comforted in our trials, but that our trials can equip us to comfort others. I was comforted by those words of the Apostle Paul, just as many others have been. The Lord knew that young romance was not His will for my life, and that I would find in Ruth the perfect wife for me.

Pious Platitudes Don't Help

An overdose of Scripture at the wrong time may do more harm than good. Hearing verses on "counting trials as joy," in the midst of someone's difficulty can be like throwing gasoline on a fire or rubbing salt in a wound. A person needs time to assimilate what has happened, to assess the physical or emotional damage. Hearing something like "God must love you very much to put you through this," is not the bandage a person needs.

We need to build trust through listening, through caring in a tangible way. Perhaps your friend doesn't know the Lord, and you feel awkward bringing up the subject of God as the one who comforts perfectly. You might say, "I wish I could do more for you. When you feel like it, let me take you to lunch."

If you cannot find examples in your life that might relate to a sufferer, the perfect example is Jesus. He experienced people who betrayed Him. He knows what it is like to suffer. You can explain how your hurting friend can have a relationship with Him. Pray for the right words, pray for the way to comfort. Pray, don't preach.

Who Are the Best Comforters?

Those who have suffered most are often best able to comfort others. I know of pastors whose ministries have been enriched by suffering. Through their trials they have learned to live through the difficulties of people in their church family.

Someone who has experienced the same sort of pain is the one who can minister best. However, to say, "I know how you feel," is usually an unnecessary and frequently unwelcome approach. No one knows exactly how another feels. One couple who had lost their oldest son in an accident tried to comfort another couple whose child had died after lingering for many months. The comfort was only in the loss, not in the circumstances. Better to say, "I don't know how you feel, I can't really put myself in your shoes, but this is how I was comforted . . ." Our sufferings may be hard to bear, but they teach us lessons which, in turn, equip and enable us to help others.

"

Our sufferings may be hard to bear,
but they teach us lessons
which, in turn,
equip and enable us to help others.

"

Only God's spirit can truly mend a broken heart, but we can be a part of the healing process. We don't have to be a priest or preacher, a trained counselor or psychiatrist to be a comforter. We just need to be available, as Christ is available to us. When He was comforting His disciples before He left them, they were confused, questioning, and frightened. He said, "Now is your time of grief, but I will see you again and you will rejoice, and no one will take away your joy" (John 16:22).

Our attitude toward suffering should not be, "Grit your teeth and bear it," hoping it will pass as quickly as possible. Our goal should be to learn all we can from our personal problems, so that we can fulfill a ministry of comfort, just as Jesus did. "Because he himself suffered when he was tempted, he is able to help those who are being tempted" (Hebrews 2:18).

We are surrounded by hurting people. Some may wear a plastic mask, but beneath the mask is a scarred soul. Are we approachable and available, even when we may be hurting, too? God does not comfort us to make us comfortable, but to make us comforters.

14

Schoolroom for Heaven

Why, you do not even know what will happen tomorrow. What is your life? You are a mist that appears for a little while and then vanishes.

James 4:14

IN MILAN, ITALY, A CITY KNOWN FOR ITS ART, there is an impressive cathedral that has some significant words inscribed around its entrance. To the right of the door is a sculptured wreath of roses. Underneath it says: "All that pleases us is only for a moment." On the left is a sculptured cross of thorns with these words beneath: "All that troubles us is only for a moment." Over the top are the words, "Nothing is important but that which is eternal."

Our pleasures are so brief. The vacation is over too soon, the fashionable suit wears out, the ice cream cone melts. Likewise, we may believe that our pain will never stop, the pressure in our lives will have no end. But someday, both the pleasures and the pain of life on earth will be over.

Someone said, "Live each day as if it's your last. It may be." A group of people were sitting on a bench at the Los Angeles airport. They were waiting for the shuttle to take them to the parking lot where they had left their cars. Suddenly the brakes gave way on the bus they were to board, and it plunged into the benches, killing one woman and injuring others. The husband of the dead woman, who had been sitting beside her, jumped clear and was saved.

I sometimes wonder, when I hear of sudden fatalities, if the victims were prepared for death. Every day we hear of such happenings. People who in an instant of time are transferred from this life to the next. The Bible has much to say about the brevity of life and the necessity of preparing for eternity. We all need to prepare for the final exams in the schoolroom for Heaven.

I Don't Want to Think About It

When Scarlett O'Hara wanted to avoid a decision, she would say, "I'll think about it tomorrow." Too many Christians avoid thinking about death, because somehow they think the subject is unpleasant. Death is Satan's weapon, for he uses the thought of it to bring confusion and fear into the hearts of those facing it.

We need to remember that death is not of God, it is part of the curse sin brought on this world and which has the universe in its grasp. The good news is that for Christians death is not final. It is another phase of life. When a Christian dies, he moves immediately into a glorious eternal life. The Bible says, "Death has been swallowed up in victory" (1 Corinthians 15:54). I believe that if people paid more attention to death, eternity, and judgment, there would be more holy living on earth.

Surrounded by the violence and devastation of our present age, we see death on every hand, but it never seems real until we stare it in the face ourselves, or hold the hand of someone who is slipping into eternity.

The Christian knows he has eternal life, "And this is the testimony: God has given us eternal life, and this life is in his Son. He who has the Son has life; he who does not have the Son of God does not have life" (1 John 5:11–12).

Those who do not have Jesus Christ in their hearts will spend eternity separated from God. The Bible has a great deal to say about Hell, although until recent times the subject has all but disappeared from our modern pulpits. However, it was reported in a major newsmagazine that Hell is making a major comeback in American thinking.

A poll showed that of the younger Americans (between the ages of eighteen and twenty-nine), 84 percent believed in Heaven and 71 percent believed in Hell. Older Americans, aged fifty and up, were not so definite; 74 percent believed in Heaven, and 54 percent believed in Hell. It was said that three out of five Americans now believe in Hell. This is a decided increase over similar polls taken in previous years. Why this comeback? Martin Marty, a chronicler of American religious trends, said, "If people really believed in hell . . . they'd be out rescuing people."[1]

Many who are cynical about the Christian faith think deeply about life and eternity. The same Gallup poll revealed that 61 percent of those who claimed to have no religion believed they were going to Heaven and 83 percent of those who attend church believed they would be in Heaven.

We have seen thousands accept Christ for the first time who have been attending church for years. It has been said that being born in a garage does not make you an automobile, or, as Corrie ten Boom so colorfully said, "A mouse in a cookie jar isn't a cookie."

The schoolroom for Heaven has some wonderful classes and inspiring teachers. Some of the courses should be required for credit.

Is Your House in Order?

If we accept that someday, sooner or later, we are going to face death, should we be making preparations while we are living? Hezekiah, a king of Israel, was a very sick man when Isaiah the prophet went to him and said, "Put your house in order, because you are going to die" (Isaiah 38:1).

I am not a prophet, but that was certainly good advice. Too many have neglected to put their houses in order, and as a result, those who are left have had burdens added to heartache. From a practical standpoint, if we have any earthly possessions, have we made our wills? How old are they? A will should be updated every few years as children grow and circumstances change. When my father-in-law, Dr. Nelson Bell, died, his estate was in such order, with documents neatly filed in folders and explicit instructions for the distribution of his possessions, that there was no confusion. He was a great inspiration to me both in life and in his preparation for death.

How much time do we have? King Hezekiah was given a fifteen-year extension on his life. Many of us are given reprieves. The doctor may say, "You'll probably live another twenty years or more." God may not be finished with us yet. But even the best of medical knowledge cannot determine the days of our lives.

The Scripture teaches us that God knows the exact moment when each person is to die. "All the days ordained for me were written in your book before one of them came to be" (Psalm 139:16). And Job 14:5 reads, "Man's days are determined; you have decreed the number of his months and have set limits he cannot exceed."

Our days are numbered. One of the primary goals in our lives should be to prepare for the day on which our number is up. The legacy we leave is not just in our possessions, but in the quality of our lives. What preparations should we be making now? The greatest waste in all of our earth, which cannot be recycled or reclaimed, is our waste of the time God has given us each day.

Golden Minutes of Opportunity

We are told to "Be very careful, then, how you live—not as unwise but as wise, making the most of every opportunity, because the days are evil" (Ephesians 5:15–16). If we knew this was our last day on earth, what opportunities would we use? Call a friend who was hurting? Say "I'm sorry" to someone we've slighted? Encourage a young person who was struggling with a school or job? Tell our husband or wife, parents or children, how much we love them? Most important, would we tell someone about Jesus Christ and how they could have eternal life through Him? How would we spend those final twenty-four hours?

> "*The greatest waste in all of our earth is our waste of the time God has given us each day.*"

One woman who knew the exact time of her death was Velma Barfield. Velma was a convicted murderer, a woman who had committed heinous crimes while under the addiction of many different drugs. She was in a security prison, awaiting trial, when she heard a radio evangelist who said that no matter what she had done, Jesus loved her and wanted to come into her heart and give her a new spirit. Although she had heard those words all of her life, for the first time she truly understood them. Velma became a new creature in Christ while waiting for her death sentence.

For the next six years, through the love of people who cared, Velma grew in her knowledge of God. It was during this time that she wrote my wife, Ruth, and they began to correspond. Our daughter Anne, who lives in the same city where the prison was located, went to visit Velma, and she was present at her execution in 1984.

Velma Barfield was a great influence for good on many people in and outside of prison. Anne told us, "On three separate occasions Velma told me, 'If I had the choice of living free on the outside without my Lord, or living on death row with Him, I would choose death row.' As November 2 (the day of her execution) drew closer, her increasing desire to see the face of her beloved Lord took the sting of fear away."[2]

Anne and Ruth told me that Velma had been praying for a year and a half for a revival to take place within the prison population. A month after her execution I led a service at the prison. And 210 inmates and staff members responded to the invitation to receive Christ. Afterward I walked into the very cellblock where Velma had been housed for three years. I found the inmates, who did not know that I was coming, with their Bibles open, watching a television broadcast of one of our Crusades. Velma's witness, even after her death, continued to permeate the place where she lived. Today a woman's Bible class carries on—a result of Velma's life.

What an Opportunity!

I didn't breeze through school. Studying was hard for me, and exam time was terrifying. But when I got my diploma, it looked just like the one that the valedictorian received. Perhaps his had a few more ribbons on it, but I graduated just the same.

Life is a glorious schoolroom to prepare us for graduation. It may be very tough, and we may fail some of the tests. But all the preparation is worth it to get the rewards at the end.

Fanny Crosby was a woman who was given a difficult course. She was blinded in infancy as the result of negligence on the part of a doctor. To compensate for the loss of her sight, she keenly developed other senses, and she became one of the greatest hymn writers ever. One of her most beautiful hymns, "I Shall See Him Face to Face," might never have been written were it not for the fact that she had never looked upon green fields, an evening sunset, or her mother's face. It was the loss of her vision that helped her gain her remarkable spiritual discernment.

The Living Bible says, "These troubles and suffering of ours are, after all, quite small and won't last very long. Yet this short time of distress will result in God's richest blessing upon us forever and ever!" (2 Corinthians 4:17).

I can still remember how long school seemed to be. Would summer vacation ever come? Would finals ever be over? Summer always came, and finals always ended. Life is just a schoolroom with a glorious opportunity to prepare us for eternity. If we fail in this, though we succeed in everything else, our life will have been a failure.

What Is Death?

The question, "What is life all about?" is frequently heard, especially by young people who are just beginning their lives. Seldom do we hear people ask, "What is death all about?" And yet one follows the other. In *King Lear,* Shakespeare said, "Fear of death is worse than death itself."

I have faced death many times, and my reactions have not always been the same. One time I had an operation that almost ended me. I knew this could be serious, so before they wheeled me into the operating room I called two of my closest friends and gave them instructions about my wife, my family, and my ministry. Ruth had gone to be with the children, and I tried to keep the seriousness of the situation from her. Whether this was right or wrong, I don't know. At least I'm living to tell the story.

I remember alternating between two feelings. First, the complete peace I had, knowing that I would be with my Lord Jesus Christ, and second, the fear of leaving my loved ones. I certainly thought I was going to die.

But the Lord wasn't finished with me. Death for a Christian is not an accident. The Bible says, "Precious in the sight of the Lord is the death of his saints" (Psalm 116:15 KJV).

How could there be anything precious about death? When a child or a young person dies, the tragedy seems so much greater than for someone who has lived a long life. People begin to question why God would allow such a thing. Do you think that God, whose "eye is on the sparrow" and who knows the very numbers of the hairs on our heads, would turn His back on one of His children in the hour of peril?

Paul lived most of his life on the brink of death. When his tired, bruised body began to weaken under the punishment he received, he said triumphantly, "We know that if the earthly tent we live in is destroyed, we have a building from God, an eternal house in heaven, not built by human hands" (2 Corinthians 5:1).

One of my dear friends had a son who was killed at the age of eighteen in a plane crash. On his gravestone are the words, "To me, to live is Christ and to die is gain" (Philippians 1:21).

What is death? For the Christian, death is a friend rather than an enemy. It is another step on the pathway to Heaven rather than a leap into some dark unknown.

How Do We Know There Is Life After Death?

If we have never died, how do we know there is hope for eternal life? Can we be certain there is life after death? Yes! There is one great fact that gives the Christian assurance in the face of death: *the resurrection of Jesus Christ*. This truth is the basis for our belief, for our living, and for our hope. The resurrection of Christ is the central event of all history.

"

Because Christ rose from the dead, we know there is life after death, and that if we belong to Him we need not fear death.

"

One of the great biblical scholars was my friend, Wilbur Smith. He wrote:

> If you or I should say to any group of friends that we expected to die, either by violence or naturally, at a certain time, but that, three days after death, we would rise again, we would be quietly taken away by friends and confined to an institution until our minds became clear and sound again.
>
> This would be right, for only a foolish man would go around talking about rising from the dead on the third day, only a foolish man, unless he knew that this was going to take place, and no one in the world has ever known that about himself except One Christ, the Son of God.[3]

Because Christ rose from the dead, we know that sin and death and Satan have been defeated. Because Christ rose from the dead, we know there is life after death, and that if we belong to Him we need not fear death. Jesus said, "I am the resurrection and the life. He who believes in me will live, even though he dies; and whoever lives and believes in me will never die" (John 11:25–26).

Christians do not die. They go on living in another realm; a place so wonderful that I can only try to describe it in the next chapter. In fact, that's what life after death is: another chapter in our personal biography, written by "Jesus, the author and perfecter of our faith" (Hebrews 12:2).

Someone has said that death is not a period, but a comma in the story of life.

Death Is the Coronation of a Christian

Once there was a prince who went into a foreign land and fought a fierce enemy. He conquered the foe who was a threat to his country and returned home to be crowned and honored for what he had done. It was a magnificent coronation!

The Bible says that as long as we are here on earth, we are strangers in a foreign land. There are enemies to be conquered before we return home. This world is not our home; our citizenship is in Heaven.

There is a time coming when all Christians will stand before God and give an account of the way they used the gifts God has given them. It will be a time of truth for all believers. There are different crowns that are available, and these are given according to the quality of work we have done on earth.

For those who have endured trials and suffering with patience, there is a special crown of life. James 1:12 says, "Blessed is the man who perseveres under trial, because when he has stood the test, he will receive the crown of life."

For those who believe the only rewards worth desiring are measured by what money can buy, there will be surprises in Heaven to see who will receive some of the special crowns.

Death Is a Rest

God's people do not enjoy much rest here on earth. In recent years we have heard the term "burn-out" more often.

Some accomplish more in a few years than others do in a lifetime, but someday their toil will come to an end. The Bible says, "There remains, then, a Sabbath-rest for the people of God; for anyone who enters God's rest also rests from his own work, just as God did from his" (Hebrews 4:9–10).

We may get some rest on earth, but heavenly rest will be so refreshing that we will never feel that exhaustion of mind and body we so frequently experience now. I'm really looking forward to that.

Death Is a Departure

Ruth and I have said good-bye many times in our life together. Sometimes we were separated by oceans and time differences. When I leave her there is always a tinge of sadness, because she is the one I love more than any other person on earth. But we part in the sure hope that we shall meet again.

The word *departure* literally means to pull up anchor and set sail. Everything that happens prior to death is a preparation for the final voyage. Death marks the beginning, not the end. It is our journey to God.

The believing Christian has hope as he stands at the grave of a loved one who is with the Lord, for he knows that the separation is not forever. It is a glorious truth that those who are in Christ never see each other for the last time.

A poet said:

> Wish me "Bon Voyage!"
> As you do a friend
> Whose joyous visit finds its happy end.
> And bid me both "a Dieu!"
> And "au revoir!"
> Since, though I come no more,
> I shall be waiting there to greet you,
> At His Door.[4]

Death Is a Transition

When former President John Quincy Adams was eighty years old, he was met by an old friend who shook his trembling hand and said, "Good morning. How is John Quincy Adams today?"

The retired chief executive looked at him for a moment and then said, "John Quincy Adams himself is quite well, sir, quite well, but the house in which he lives at present is becoming dilapidated. It is tottering upon its foundations. Time and the seasons have almost destroyed it. Its roof is pretty worn out. Its walls are much shattered, and it crumbles with every wind. The old tenement is becoming almost uninhabitable, and I think that John Quincy Adams will have to move out of it soon. But he himself is well, sir, quite well!"

It was not long afterward that he had his second and fatal stroke, and John Quincy Adams moved from his "shaky tabernacle," as he called it, to his "house not made with hands."

To the Christian, death is the exchanging of a tent for a building. If our earthly tent is disintegrating, or if it has many structural imperfections, someday we will be given the title to a home that will never deteriorate.

Joni Eareckson Tada will walk and run again. Helen Keller will see and hear. The child who died of cancer will have rosy cheeks and a strong body. The man crippled with arthritis will stand upright. The woman who was disfigured in a fiery car crash will have a face without blemish. Everything that we try to change, paint, and correct on earth will have a glorious new look. And yet we will know each other in our heavenly bodies!

Death Is Different for the Believer

C. S. Lewis said, "I have seen great beauty of spirit in some who were great sufferers. I have seen men, for the most part, grow better not worse with advancing years, and I have seen the last illness produce treasures of fortitude and meekness from most unpromising subjects."[5]

There is something decidedly different about the death of a believer. No wonder Paul said, "I desire to depart and be with Christ, which is better by far" (Philippians 1:23).

I have talked to doctors and nurses who have held the hands of dying people, and they say there is often as much difference between the death of a Christian and a non-Christian as there is between Heaven and Hell.

The words said by dying saints before they went to Heaven have inspired me. My grandmother sat up in her bed, smiled, and said, "I see Jesus and His hand outstretched to me. And there is Ben, and he has both of his eyes and both of his legs." (Ben, my grandfather, had lost a leg and an eye at the battle of Gettysburg.)

John Knox said, "Live in Christ, die in Christ, and the flesh need not fear death."

John Wesley said, "The best of all is, God is with us."

When Joseph Everett was dying, he said, "Glory! Glory! Glory!" and he continued exclaiming glory for over twenty-five minutes. What do you suppose he was experiencing?

Victor Hugo said, "The nearer I approach to the end, the plainer I hear around me the immortal symphonies of the worlds which invite me."

The writer of "Rock of Ages," Augustus Toplady, was triumphant as he lay dying at the age of thirty-eight. "I enjoy Heaven already in my soul," he said, "my prayers are all converted into praises."

The Rev. and Mrs. R. Porteous were taken prisoners by Chinese communist bandits in 1931, and led to a lonely spot on top of a hill where they were to be executed. The leader said, "This is the place." The executioner took a long knife from its holder and raised it above the necks of the courageous couple. Certain death seemed imminent. However, instead of cringing and begging for mercy, the couple began to sing. The bandits stared open-mouthed as they heard this hymn:

Face to face with Christ, my Savior,
Face to face—what will it be?
When with rapture I behold him,
Jesus Christ who died for me.

These two saintly souls were ready for death and thought that would be their last song. But to their surprise, no order was given. The executioner returned the knife to its place, and the couple was released. Subsequently, they told the story of the perfect peace that the Lord Jesus gave to them in the face of certain death.

Jesus Gave Us the Key

John Milton said, "Death is the golden key that opens the palace of eternity." What is that place like? Is Heaven worth dying for?

15

No More Troubles

One hour of eternity, one moment with the Lord, will make us utterly forget a lifetime of desolations.

Horatius Bonar

HE WAS JUST A LITTLE BOY, ONLY TEN YEARS OLD, but Russell Davis knew what it was to live a life of pain. For four years he fought a battle with cancer. One Saturday, when he was back in the hospital again, he wrote this note to his best friend:

> Dear Brian. How are you doing? I'm alright in the hospital but a little sleepy. I know that you worry about me some but don't worry too much. Also if it will help you feel better you can come see me if you have time.
>
> When I die, if I do soon, don't worry 'cause I'll be somewhere special in Heaven. And sooner than I know it you'll be up in Heaven with me 'cause a thousand years on earth is a minute in Heaven.
>
> I know you'll miss me when I'm gone but just accept it like you did with your uncle. My mom will give you something of mine so you can remember me always. So don't worry too much. Love, Russell.

Three days later, Russell asked for a sip of water and said, "I love you, Mom. I love you, Dad." And he went home to be with the Lord. Some people write better sermons when they die than others do in a lifetime of speaking.

We often look at a child or a young person and wonder why they weren't allowed to live out a normal life span on earth. I believe God prepares some of his precious young ones in order that they may have an influence on their peers at an age when they are forming the direction of their lives. The Bible says, "His loved ones are very precious to him and he does not lightly let them die" (Psalm 116:15 TLB).

We wonder, how can there be anything precious about death? God knows that after we've served our purpose here there is something much greater waiting for us. The younger God takes one of His children, the more dramatically it points people to the reality of Christ.

Where Is Heaven?

Heaven is a place, not just an experience. We hear of so many things being heavenly, from a chocolate soufflé to an exotic island. But the real Heaven is our eternal home.

Jesus said, "I am going there to prepare a place for you. And if I go . . . I will come back and take you to be with me that you also may be where I am" (John 14:2–3). That place is beyond anything we have on earth or anything man can build. Heaven is "my Father's house." Before Jesus went to the cross, He gathered His disciples in the upper room and talked about a home. He said, "In my Father's house are many rooms" (John 14:2). In the King James Version, it says "many mansions." This does not mean an imposing house, but a resting place. Heaven is a place of rest. If I tell the Lord I'm tired when I arrive in His house, He'll say, "Rest, Billy." God rested on the seventh day of Creation, so it is not incompatible with His will to tell us to rest. But there will be activity, too. My idea of Heaven is working forever and never getting tired. Heaven will not be an eternal Sunday afternoon nap.

When we are young we may long to get away from home and be out on our own. We want freedom from parental rules and restrictions. But when the storms of life flatten us, we may yearn to go back to the security of home. The home of our memories may not exist, or the safety we once knew in that place may be gone. Heaven will give us security and safety forever.

Some believers are lying on hospital beds today. Some may be suffering from terrible diseases or be in prisons or labor camps. They long for home, where they may find relief from their pain and a new sense of love in their lives. The home and the love that is waiting for them is Jesus Christ Himself, and because of Him, Heaven at last and forever!

"

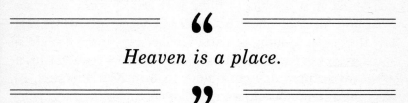

Heaven is a place.

"

When death stares us in the face, our life after death takes on new importance. Phil Manly, the chaplain of the huge USC Medical Center in Los Angeles, has hundreds of stories about the harvest of souls at hospitals. He said, "A fifty-eight-year-old lady with cancer, whose life nearly ended twice during a medical crisis, asked the Lord to change her into His image; another young man who was terrified upon learning that he had AIDS, asked to speak with the Chaplain and received the Lord that same evening; a young man and his wife received the Lord in the burn ward. He had attempted to set an individual's car on fire as an act of revenge and ended up badly burned himself."

All of us must prepare to meet God while we are still living. Someday everyone will stand before His throne and give an account of himself or herself. The saddest words I can ever imagine would be to hear the Lord say, "I never knew you. Away from me" (Matthew 7:23).

Beautiful Home and Gardens

When spring comes to our mountain home, my wife heads for the garden. She has always kept a home of comfort and beauty for our family. When I am in yet another hotel room in some city around the world, I often think of our mountain home, filled with a lifetime of memories and love.

Imagine some of the most beautiful places in the world. Switzerland when the sun breaks over the snow-capped peaks and spills onto the slopes filled with wildflowers. A crystal clear lake, nestled among pine trees. A beach with white sand and the gentle lapping of warm Caribbean waters. A night in the desert west with a million stars against a velvet backdrop. An autumn day on a quiet road in New England. An easy chair, a good book, a cup of hot chocolate, and a glowing fire when the snow is falling at home.

Heaven will be more than that, because it is the Father's house, and He is a God of beauty. The same hand that made the beauty of this world has a more beautiful place prepared for us.

Man has polluted so much of our earth, but in Heaven there will be no environmental concerns. The water will be pure, the air clean, and there will be no need for landfills or recycled paper and cans.

In Revelation, when John caught a glimpse of Heaven, the only thing he could think to compare it to was a bride on her wedding day. I have three daughters and two daughters-in-law, and every one was a beautiful bride, but their beauty was just a dim reflection of Heaven.

If we are amazed and thrilled when we view some of the beauty the Lord gave us on earth, I'm sure we are in for some wonderful surprises in Heaven.

Happiness Is Heaven

I know many beautiful homes that are unhappy. If we look around us, or look within us, we know that we are basically living on an unhappy planet. Stand on any street corner in the large cities of the world and watch faces. When we get to Heaven, all the elements that made for unhappiness on earth will be gone. Think of a place where there is no sin, no sorrow, no insecurities, no quarrels, no selfishness, no racism, no misunderstandings, no hurt feelings, no worries, no pain, no sickness, no suffering, no death.

Heaven will be filled with music and song. Its citizens will sing a "new song," giving glory to Jesus Christ, who was slain and redeemed "men for God from every tribe and language and people and nation" (Revelation 5:9).

> "*The same hand that made the beauty of this world has a more beautiful place prepared for us.*"

We are told that a mighty chorus will sing, "Hallelujah! For our Lord God Almighty reigns" (Revelation 19:6). Handel's Messiah sung by the greatest choirs on earth cannot compare with the heavenly chorus. When Bev Shea sings at our Crusades, as he has since the beginning, I am blessed as no other singer blesses me. Heaven will resound with voices like his.

No Boredom

Heaven will be a place where we have work to do. It may be the kind of work we have never experienced on earth. No frustrations, no freeways, no failure or fatigue. Cliff Barrows, our song director, and Bev Shea, our special soloist, have been with me for forty years. They occasionally tease me by saying that when we get to Heaven, I'll be out of work, but they won't!

Have you ever done anything that was so exhilarating, so rewarding, that you hoped it would never end? It's been said that no work is so wearisome as doing nothing. In Heaven our work will be stimulating and rewarding.

In Revelation 22:3, John wrote: "His servants will serve him." Each one of us will be given some task that we will enjoy doing. Some may be the cooks who prepare heavenly dishes, some may play with the children. Perhaps we will be called upon to tend the gardens or polish the rainbows. Our imaginations are limitless. Whatever we do, the Bible says we will serve Him. Just think—loving the work you are doing and never getting tired!

The Ultimate Family Reunion

Have you ever been in a strange place and had the joy of seeing a familiar face? No one who enters the Father's house will feel lonely or strange, for our friends will be there. We may be very surprised by whom we meet.

My wife is fond of the following little poem she picked up somewhere. She has no idea who wrote it, or where it comes from.

> When you get to Heaven
> You will doubtless view
> Many whose presence there
> Will be a shock to you.
> Do not look around
> Do not even stare

Doubtless there'll be many
Surprised to see you there.

If you are a believer, you will see those friends and family who accepted Christ. Our family reunion will have all the people from the Bible you always wanted to know. The Old and New Testament saints will be there to greet you and answer some of those questions you always wanted to ask. We won't have to rush or stand in line, for we will have all of eternity to enjoy.

The Head of the House

God's house will be happy because Christ will be there. Life with Christ is endless love; without Him it is a loveless end. In Revelation 22 we are told that we "will see his face." We have looked at paintings and seen movies that have tried to depict the face and body of Jesus. No one knows what He looks like, except those believers who are now with Him.

"

There will be millions of
Christians in Heaven,
but Jesus will know
each one of us personally,
and we shall know Him
in a deeper way than ever before.

"

Have you ever been in a crowd and stretched to see some important dignitary? Have you been at a meeting or a retreat where you hoped the speaker would recognize you? There will be millions of Christians in Heaven, but Jesus will know each one of us personally, and we shall know Him in a deeper way than ever before. "Now we see but a poor reflection as in a mirror; then we shall see face to face. Now I know in part; then I shall know fully, even as I am fully known" (1 Corinthians 13:12).

God knows our hearts. Nothing is hidden from His sight. We are "fully known" by Him, but many times He seems so remote from us. He is the "God who is there," but He does not seem real. In Heaven we will know Him in all of His glory.

But I Love Earth

There is nothing wrong with loving life, in fact we should enjoy it to the hilt. In Heaven, we will enjoy everything more. Paul said, "For to me, to live is Christ and to die is gain" (Philippians 1:21).

What will we gain? I can only imagine that whatever we loved on earth will be magnified in its pleasure in Heaven.

We may not be married in Heaven. Some of us who love our wives or husbands very much may find that sad, but the more I think about the promises of Heaven, the more I believe whatever God has in store for us will be unbelievably more joyous, more delightful, and more wonderful than what we now enjoy.

I trust Jesus with my eternal tomorrows and know that He will solve all of the questions we have now. We will be able to understand one another, for there will be one universal language, the language of love, that will enable us to talk freely with people who lived in other earth countries. The "communication gap" will be closed.

Night comes on earth, filled with darkness and peril. In many cities on our planet we are warned not to go out on the streets at night. But in Heaven, there is no night. We will not need to sleep, because on earth sleep is to restore our strength. But in Heaven there will be no energy drains, so sleep will not be necessary.

Night is a time when many crimes are committed. In Heaven, evil is gone and the light that will surround us will be a reflection of the light of the world, Jesus Christ.

Will we miss our life on earth? We won't even remember it! Isaiah said: "Behold, I will create new heavens and a new earth. *The former things will not be remembered, nor will they come to mind"* (65:17, emphasis added).

Heaven Is a City

When the Book of Revelation was written, cities were places of refuge, companionship, and security. Today, they speak of crowding, crime, and corruption. Heaven as a city is the former description, not our modern concept of a city.

Revelation pictures Heaven as a city, the new Jerusalem. This is the city where we will live forever. It will be large enough to house all believers without being crowded.

> "*I believe whatever God has in store for us will be unbelievably more joyous, more delightful, and more wonderful than what we now enjoy.*"

For centuries women have loved jewels. The New Jerusalem will have gates of pearl, streets of gold, and the foundations of the city walls will be like a display case at Tiffany's, multiplied many times in their magnificence.

On Main Street in New Jerusalem, the Tree of Life will be growing. Everyone will have access to it. John describes the Tree of Life as "bearing twelve crops of fruit, yielding its fruit every month. And the leaves of the tree are for the healing of the nations" (Revelation 22:2). The Tree of Life will accomplish what the United Nations, heads of state, ambassadors, and peace-making missions have never been able to do. Harmony will reign in Heaven.

My wife and I do not like cities. We do not care for "mansions." We love log houses, on the primitive side, with simple comforts. Could it be that each will see through his or her own eyes, differently from others—what will look like a jeweled city to some will appear to others like log cabins scattered over mountains and coves?

The struggle to support our families has been increasingly difficult. Inflation, taxes, high insurance rates, and many other drains on our personal finances have had damaging effects on our lives. Money will not be a worry in Heaven, in fact, there won't be any. The Bible tells us to "drink without cost from the spring of the water of life" (Revelation 21:6). We will not work for wages, but for the sheer joy of creating and producing.

Full Potential

One of man's greatest insecurities is his fear of failure. Life is not a series of successes, for we fail in employment, business, personal relationships, and professional endeavors. In Heaven we will never fail. We will succeed in whatever we undertake, for "no longer will there be any curse" (Revelation 22:3). The person who never got an "A" on his report card, or a parking place with his name on it, will be just as important as the corporate executive or the concert star.

Spiritually, we will be close to God, for His people will live in His presence and praise Him continually. There will be no "dry periods" in our spiritual experience, for we shall live joyfully forever with the Lord.

I think that when we reach Heaven, we will have our potentials fully realized. When God is allowed to have full control of our lives, we will know the kind of people we can really be. On earth we use only a small part of our potential, but in Heaven we will have our God-given talents released.

Together Forever

An unknown poet wrote:

> In this dark world of sin and pain
> We only meet to part again;
> But when we reach the heavenly shore,
> We there shall meet to part no more.
> The joy that we shall see that day
> Shall chase our present griefs away.

All the glories of Heaven will be multiplied because of the people we will know there. On earth, whenever we have a great experience, we want to share it with someone else. Won't it be thrilling to share Heaven with our children, our parents, our friends, and all of the great people who have gone before us?

The Final Victory

In this present world we are in the midst of a battlefield. We can understand Paul when he spoke of being harassed at every turn—conflicts on the outside, fears within (2 Corinthians 7:5).

In the battle of life, we are in a wrestling match, not only with flesh and blood, but also with principalities and powers, with the rulers of darkness and spiritual wickedness. We wonder if we will ever be "on top of it." All children of God will find songs of victory at the end. All war-weary soldiers will be able to rest.

Whenever I see an athlete come from behind and take the gold medal, or a team that is the underdog score the winning points with only seconds to go, I think of what Paul said. "I have fought the good fight, I have finished the race, I have kept the faith. Now there is in store for me the crown of righteousness, which the Lord, the righteous Judge, will award to me on that day" (2 Timothy 4:7–8).

Many stories are told and books written about aliens visiting our planet. Christians are really aliens who land for a while on this earth and then go to their true home. In the days before his death, Paul looked forward with great anticipation to the time when he would finally receive his crown of glory. We should live as Paul did, serving faithfully and anticipating Christ's return, whether that be to catch us up to be with Him in the clouds, or whether we go to see Him before that.

A few more days may dawn and darken and we will know the unending day. A few brief years, or brief moments, and we shall enter that eternal city, sit in the shadow of the Tree of Life, and drink the crystal clear water. We have only had a foretaste on earth of what it means to love and be loved.

Are you ready? I know that I am prepared to meet the Master, not because of preaching or books, but because one day, many years ago, I confessed my sins and asked the Lord to come into my life and make of me what He wanted.

That is one decision no one will regret, either in this life or in the one to come. "I consider that our present sufferings are not worth comparing with the glory that will be revealed in us" (Romans 8:18).

A Voice from Beyond

We were in Seattle for a Crusade after the end of the war in the Persian Gulf. President Bush had proclaimed March 7, 1991, as a day of celebration for the liberation of Kuwait and the end of hostilities in the Gulf. We had invited a lady to speak to the thousands of people at that meeting. I'm sure she must have been nervous, but she told a story that touched us all.

Here is part of what Mrs. Shirley Lansing said:

> I come with a story about my son, John Kendall Morgan, Warrant Officer One, United States Army, serving in Operation Desert Storm. Jack committed his life to Jesus when he was young. . . . At the time it didn't seem terribly important, but it was. A few weeks ago, two officers came to our door and told us they regretted to inform us that our son had been killed in action when his helicopter was shot down by hostile Iraqi fire.
>
> When Jack got on the airplane to leave for Saudi Arabia, he gave Lisa, his fiancé, a bride's book, so they could be planning the wedding. I speak to you only from my heart, and out of my pain, because only God can give me the strength to stand here before you and say these words. But they're so important. Each of you has the decision to make that my son made. And this is a time when you have a choice and we never know how long we'll have to make that decision.
>
> Three weeks before he was killed, Jack wrote two letters, to be opened "just in case." After we got the news, we opened our letter and it said, "In case you have to open this, please don't worry. I am all right. . . . *Now I know something you don't know—what heaven's like!*"

And someday *we* will know, too.

Notes

Chapter 1—World in Pain

1. *Time,* 3 December 1990, 45.
2. Ibid., 46.
3. *U.S. News & World Report,* 24 September 1990, 37.
4. *Time,* 7 May 1990, 92.
5. Ibid., 99.
6. Francis Schaeffer, *Pollution and the Death of Man* (Wheaton, Ill.: Tyndale House, 1970), 10–11.
7. Aleksandr Solzhenitsyn, *The Gulag Archipelago* (New York: Harper & Row, 1973), 3–4.
8. *Los Angeles Times,* 12 October 1990, A13.
9. Russell Chandler, *Understanding the New Age* (Dallas: Word Publishing, 1988), 104.
10. Horatius Bonar, *When God's Children Suffer* (Grand Rapids, Mich.: Kregel Publications, 1981), preface.

Chapter 2—His Unfailing Love

1. Lloyd Ogilvie, *Ask Him Anything* (Dallas: Word Publishing, 1981), 13.
2. Francis Schaeffer, *The Mark of the Christian* (Downers Grove, Ill.: Inter-Varsity, 1976), 28.
3. Richard Wurmbrand, *In God's Underground* (New York: Fawcett World Library, 1968), 249.

Chapter 3—Into Each Life Some Rain . . .

1. Charles Colson, *Against the Night* (Ann Arbor, Mich.: Servant Book, 1989), 165.

Chapter 5—Why Jesus Suffered

1. Philip Yancey, *Where Is God When It Hurts?* (Grand Rapids, Mich.: Zondervan, 1990), 156.

Chapter 6—Who Sinned?

1. H. L. Ellison, *A Study of Job* (Grand Rapids, Mich.: Zondervan, 1971), 19.
2. Philip Yancey, *Where Is God When It Hurts?* (Grand Rapids, Mich.: Zondervan, 1990), 89.
3. Charles Colson, *The God of Stones and Spiders* (Wheaton, Ill.: Crossway Books, 1990), 99.

Chapter 7—Why God's Children Suffer

1. C.S. Lewis, *The Problem of Pain* (New York: Macmillan, 1955), 93.
2. Horatius Bonar, *When God's Children Suffer* (Grand Rapids, Mich.: Kregel Publications, 1981), 28.
3. Clebe McClary with Diane Barker, *Living Proof* (Pawleys Island, S.C.: Clebe McClary, 1978), 140.
4. *Lines to Live By* (Nashville: Thomas Nelson, 1972), 162.
5. Corrie ten Boom, *A Prisoner and Yet* (London: Christian Literature Crusade, 1954).

Chapter 8—What Do I Do When I Hurt?

1. Oswald Chambers, *My Utmost for His Highest* (Westwood, N.J.: Barbour & Co., 1963), 32.
2. *Los Angeles Times,* 16 February, 1990, C9.
3. Amy Carmichael, *Rose from Brier* (Fort Washington, Pa.: Christian Literature Crusade, 1973), 12.

Chapter 9—When Your Heart Is Breaking

1. Doug Sparks, *Hope for the Hurting* (Colorado Springs, Colo.: Navpress, 1990), 6.

2. Barbara Johnson, *Stick a Geranium in Your Hat and Be Happy* (Dallas: Word Publishing, 1990), 41.
3. Ibid., 57.
4. *Los Angeles Times,* 16 February, 1991, A5.
5. David Jeremiah with C. C. Carlson, *Exposing the Myths of Parenthood* (Dallas: Word Publishing, 1988), 4.
6. David Jacobsen, "Remember Them," *Guideposts,* March 1991.
7. Mrs. Charles E. Cowman, *Streams in the Desert* (Grand Rapids, Mich.: Zondervan, 1966), 314.
8. Jay Kesler, *The Strong Weak People* (Wheaton, Ill.: Victor Books, 1977), 17.

Chapter 10—The Fourth Man in the Fire

1. Corrie ten Boom, *He Sets the Captive Free* (Old Tappan, N.J.: Fleming H. Revell, 1977), 18–19.
2. Dale Evans Rogers, *Trials, Tears, and Triumphs* (Old Tappan, N.J.: Fleming H. Revell, 1977), 118.

Chapter 11—How to Pray Through the Pain

1. Amy Carmichael, *Edges of His Ways* (London: Christian Literature Crusade, 1955), 92.
2. Doug Sparks, *Hope for the Hurting* (Colorado Springs, Colo.: Navpress, 1990), 16, 17.
3. Ruth Bell Graham, *Legacy of a Pack Rat* (Nashville, Tenn.: Oliver-Nelson Books, 1989), 151.
4. *Guideposts,* July 1990, 9.
5. Norman Vincent Peale, *How to Handle Tough Times* (Pawling, N.Y.: Foundation for Christian Living, 1990), 28–29.
6. J. Grant Howard, *Knowing God's Will and Doing It!* (Grand Rapids, Mich.: Zondervan, 1976), 29–30.
7. Margaret Clarkson, *The Meaning of Suffering* (Grand Rapids, Mich.: Eerdmans, 1983), 98.

Chapter 12—Storing Up for the Storms

1. Bob St. John, *The Landry Legend* (Dallas: Word Publishing, 1989), 163.

2. Philip Yancey, *Where Is God When It Hurts?* (Grand Rapids, Mich.: Zondervan, 1990), 164.
3. Charles Sheldon, *In His Steps* (Grand Rapids, Mich.: Zondervan, 1967), 9.

Chapter 13—How to Help the Hurting People

1. David Jeremiah, *Overcoming Loneliness* (San Bernardino, Calif.: Here's Life Publishers, 1983), 12.
2. Philip Yancey, *Helping the Hurting* (Portland, Oreg.: Multnomah Press, 1984), 9.
3. Dr. James Dobson, *Dare to Discipline* (Wheaton, Ill.: Tyndale House, 1981), 77.
4. Franklin Graham with Jeanette Lockerbie, *Bob Pierce* (Waco, Tex.: Word Publishing, 1983), 77, 180.

Chapter 14—Schoolroom for Heaven

1. *U.S. News & World Report,* 25 March 1991, 56.
2. Velma Barfield, *Woman on Death Row* (Nashville, Tenn.: Oliver-Nelson Books, 1985), 169.
3. Wilbur Smith, *Therefore Stand: Christian Apologetics* (Grand Rapids, Mich.: Baker Book House, 1965), 364.
4. John Oxenham, "A Dieu! and Au Revoir" *Lines to Live By* (Nashville: Thomas Nelson, 1972), 81.
5. C. S. Lewis, *The Problem of Pain* (New York: Macmillan, 1955), 108.